Overcoming Sel[f]
Empowering Se[lf]

Embrace your strengths, overcome setbacks, and stay motivated by turning your goals into achievements

With every goal you reach and every setback you overcome, you are increasing your self-esteem.

All rights reserved.

Copyright © 2024 Howarth Brackin Limited

No part of this book may be reproduced, or stored in a retrieval system, or transmitted in any form or by any means, electronic, mechanical, photocopying, recording, or otherwise, without express written permission of the publisher.

Table of Contents

WITH EVERY GOAL YOU REACH AND EVERY SETBACK YOU OVERCOME, YOU ARE CRAFTING A STORY OF PERSEVERANCE, SELF-COMPASSION, AND INCREASING YOUR SELF-ESTEEM.	0
CHERRY PICK, OR DEEP DIVE?	5
CHAPTER 1: THE SILENT SABOTEURS	9
1: PROCRASTINATION: THE THIEF OF TIME	13
2: THE ROOTS OF PROCRASTINATION	22
3: THE ANATOMY OF SELF-DOUBT	28
4: THE VICIOUS CYCLE	33
5: STRATEGIES TO BEGIN BREAKING FREE	38
6: BREAKING DOWN THE BARRIERS	40
7: THE POWER OF SELF-AWARENESS	45
8: THE FIRST STEP TOWARDS CHANGE	51
CHAPTER 2: SETTING CLEAR AND ACHIEVABLE GOALS	56
1: UNDERSTANDING THE IMPORTANCE OF CLEAR GOALS	61
2: DEFINING YOUR OBJECTIVES	67
3: BREAKING DOWN GOALS INTO MANAGEABLE TASKS	72
4: CREATING A ROADMAP FOR SUCCESS	78
5: OVERCOMING OBSTACLES AND STAYING MOTIVATED	83
6: BUILDING CONFIDENCE THROUGH ACTION	89
7: TAKE OUT	95
CHAPTER 3: DEVELOPING AN ACTION PLAN	99
1: IDENTIFYING YOUR GOALS	102
2: PRIORITIZING TASKS	107
3: SETTING DEADLINES	112
4: USING PRODUCTIVITY TOOLS	116
5: CREATING A STEP-BY-STEP PLAN	121
6: IMPLEMENTING YOUR PLAN	126
7: MONITORING AND ADJUSTING YOUR PLAN	131
CHAPTER 4: BUILDING A PRODUCTIVE ROUTINE	135
1: UNDERSTANDING THE IMPORTANCE OF A ROUTINE	139
2: IDENTIFYING YOUR MOST PRODUCTIVE TIMES	145
3: SETTING PRIORITIES AND GOALS	149

4: Creating a Daily Schedule	153
5: Incorporating Breaks and Downtime	156
6: Minimizing Distractions	159
7: Establishing Morning and Evening Routines	162
8: Staying Flexible and Adapting Your Routine	166
Chapter 5: Overcoming Self-Doubt	171
1: Recognizing Self-Doubt	174
2: Challenging Negative Self-Talk	179
3: Building Self-Compassion	183
4: Setting Realistic Expectations	187
5: Seeking Support and Feedback	191
6: Taking Small Steps	195
7: Reflecting on Your Journey	199
Chapter 6: Staying Motivated	203
1: Finding Your "Why?"	207
2: Creating a Vision Board	212
3: Developing a Reward System	217
4: Maintaining a Positive Attitude	222
5: Overcoming Setbacks and Challenges	227
6: Tracking Your Progress	233
7: Adapting to Change	239
Chapter 7: Accountability and Support Systems	243
1: The Power of Accountability	246
2: Choosing an Accountability Partner	250
3: Using Technology for Support	255
4: Setting Up Regular Check-Ins	260
5: Balancing Independence and Support	265
Chapter 8: Practicing Self-Compassion	269
1: Understanding Self-Compassion	272
2: Identifying Self-Critical Thoughts	276
3: Developing a Self-Compassion Practice	280
4: Healing Through Self-Compassion	284
5: Cultivating a Positive Self-Image	288
6: Sustaining Self-Compassion Over Time	293
Chapter 9: Measuring and Celebrating Progress	297
1: The Importance of Tracking Progress	300
2: Setting Milestones and Benchmarks	304
3: Reflecting on Your Achievements	307
4: Celebrating Small Wins	311

5: ADJUSTING GOALS AND PLANS	315
CHAPTER 10: SUSTAINING LONG-TERM SUCCESS	319
1: MAINTAINING HEALTHY HABITS	322
2: BUILDING RESILIENCE	326
3: CONTINUING TO SEEK SUPPORT AND ACCOUNTABILITY	330
4: CELEBRATING MILESTONES AND SUCCESSES	334
CONCLUSION: EMBRACING YOUR NEW CONFIDENCE	338

Cherry Pick, or Deep Dive?

We are all different, some of us prefer to skip or skim read, others prefer to spend time absorbing the detail. This book allows you to do both as it is designed for you to find a topic and get the flavour of it before deciding to spend more time exploring that section.

You'll notice that many similar themes e.g.: focus on progress not perfection, goal setting, celebrating success are covered in different ways under different topics. That's because in life many of the surface issues we face have the same underlying solutions.

At the start of each chapter is a synopsis that gives a broad overview on the content. You are encouraged to use it to 'cherry pick' topics of interest. Also, each section is headed with an illustration to convey its meaning, so in times of need consider flicking through the pages and trusting your instinct to draw you to an illustration as a starting point.

Others might prefer to start at the beginning and work systematically through the topics, however, you choose to move forward on your journey we wish you joy, success and happiness.

Chapter 1:
Understanding Procrastination and Self-Doubt

This chapter delves into the root causes of procrastination and self-doubt. It explains how these issues are interrelated and how they can hinder personal and professional growth. By understanding the psychological patterns behind procrastination and self-doubt, readers will be better equipped to tackle these challenges head-on.

Chapter 2:
Setting Clear and Achievable Goals

Learn the importance of setting clear, specific, and achievable goals. This chapter provides practical tips on how to define your objectives, break them down into manageable tasks, and create a roadmap for success. Setting the right goals is the first step towards building confidence and overcoming procrastination.

Chapter 3:
Developing an Action Plan

In this chapter, we'll discover how to create an effective action plan. It includes step-by-step instructions on prioritizing tasks, setting deadlines, and using productivity tools. The focus is on taking immediate, actionable steps to start making progress towards your goals.

Chapter 4:
Building a Productive Routine

Discover how to establish a daily routine that maximizes productivity. This chapter covers techniques for time management, creating a conducive work environment, and minimizing distractions. A well-structured routine helps in maintaining consistency and momentum.

Chapter 5:
Overcoming Self-Doubt

This chapter offers strategies to combat self-doubt and build self-confidence. It includes exercises to identify and challenge negative self-talk, develop a positive mindset, and celebrate small wins. Building confidence is crucial for sustaining progress and overcoming procrastination.

Chapter 6:
Staying Motivated

Learn how to stay motivated throughout your journey. This chapter discusses the importance of finding your "why," setting up a reward system, and maintaining a positive attitude. It also includes tips on how to stay motivated during setbacks and challenges.

Chapter 7:
Accountability and Support Systems

Understand the power of accountability and support. This chapter explains how to leverage accountability partners, mentors, and support groups to keep you on track. Building a strong support system can significantly boost your confidence, productivity and self-esteem.

Chapter 8:
Practicing Self-Compassion

This chapter emphasizes the importance of self-compassion and self-care. It provides techniques for managing stress, avoiding burnout, and being kind to yourself during difficult times. Practicing self-compassion is essential for maintaining long-term motivation and confidence.

Chapter 9:
Measuring and Celebrating Progress

Discover the importance of tracking your progress and celebrating achievements. This chapter offers methods for measuring success, reflecting on growth, and adjusting goals as needed. Celebrating progress reinforces positive behaviour and boosts self-confidence.

Chapter 10:
Sustaining Long-Term Success

The final chapter focuses on sustaining the habits and strategies learned throughout the book. It provides tips for continuous improvement, adapting to changes, and maintaining a growth mindset. Sustaining long-term success ensures that the confidence and productivity gains are permanent.

Conclusion:
Embracing Your New Confidence

The book concludes with a suggestion for readers to embrace their newfound confidence and take on new challenges. It reinforces the idea that overcoming procrastination and self-doubt is a continuous journey towards greater self-esteem that leads to a more fulfilling and productive life.

Chapter 1: The Silent Saboteurs

"Welcome to the journey of transforming hesitation into action. In this opening section, we introduce the concept of procrastination and self-doubt as silent saboteurs.

We will explain the basic definitions and manifestations of procrastination and self-doubt, setting the stage for deeper exploration."

Synopsis

1: The Silent Saboteurs

Welcome to the journey of transforming hesitation into action. In this section, we explore procrastination and self-doubt as silent saboteurs. Through the story of Sarah, a talented artist whose fear of failure kept her masterpiece hidden for years, we show how these forces can hold back even the most gifted individuals. Procrastination, the act of delaying tasks, and self-doubt, the lack of confidence in one's abilities, often combine to create a powerful barrier to progress and fulfilment.

2: The Roots of Procrastination

Dive deep into the psychological roots of procrastination. Meet James, a professional whose career stagnated due to his habit of putting off important tasks. James's story highlights common triggers such as fear of failure, perfectionism, and feelings of overwhelm. We explore the science behind procrastination, explaining how the prefrontal cortex (responsible for decision-making and impulse control) battles with the limbic system (the brain's reward centre), leading to the familiar tug-of-war between immediate gratification and long-term goals.

3: The Anatomy of Self-Doubt

Uncover the anatomy of self-doubt through the story of Lisa, a writer who struggled to share her work due to her persistent inner critic. This section delves into the origins of self-doubt, including childhood experiences, societal pressures, and internalized criticism. We provide psychological insights into how self-doubt impacts our decision-making processes and erodes our confidence over time, making it harder to take decisive action.

4: The Vicious Cycle

Illustrates the vicious cycle between procrastination and self-doubt with the story of Tom, an entrepreneur who couldn't launch his startup. Procrastination often leads to feelings of inadequacy and increased self-doubt, which in turn fuels further procrastination. This destructive loop can be paralyzing. We use diagrams and real-life examples to show how this cycle perpetuates itself and offer initial strategies to begin breaking free.

5: Breaking Down the Barriers

In this section, we introduce actionable steps to overcome procrastination and self-doubt. Through Maria's story of starting a successful business, we offer practical tips like setting small, achievable goals, developing a positive mindset, and using cognitive-behavioural techniques. These strategies help readers make tangible progress and build confidence with each step.

6: The Power of Self-Awareness

This section emphasizes the importance of self-awareness in combating procrastination and self-doubt. Through Alex's story of transformation via mindfulness and self-reflection, we discuss tools like journaling, meditation, and self-assessment exercises. Self-awareness is essential for making meaningful changes and overcoming internal barriers.

7: The First Step Towards Change

The chapter concludes with a motivating call to action, encouraging a positive first step towards change. Claire's inspiring story of overcoming procrastination and self-doubt reinforces that change is possible. This section summarizes key takeaways and sets the stage for the next chapter on setting clear and achievable goals.

1: Procrastination: The Thief of Time

Imagine Sarah, a talented artist who has always been praised for her creativity and skill. From a young age, Sarah showed an exceptional ability to capture the world around her in vibrant, imaginative ways. Her teachers marvelled at her work, and her family encouraged her to pursue her passion. However, despite her talent and support, Sarah often found herself staring at a blank canvas, unable to begin her next masterpiece.

Sarah's struggle was not due to a lack of inspiration or skill. Instead, it was the work of two silent saboteurs: procrastination and self-doubt. These invisible forces lurked in the shadows of her mind, whispering doubts and delaying actions. Sarah's story is a powerful example of how even the most gifted individuals can be held back by these pervasive and often misunderstood phenomena.

Procrastination is the act of delaying or postponing tasks. It's the thief of time, stealing moments that could be spent productively and leaving a trail of unfinished projects and unmet goals. For Sarah, procrastination often manifested in the form of distractions. She would find herself tidying her studio, scrolling through social media, or even watching tutorials on painting techniques—all activities that kept her from actually painting.

At its core, procrastination is a complex behaviour rooted in psychological factors. It's not simply about poor time management or laziness. Procrastination can be a coping mechanism for dealing with negative emotions such as fear, anxiety, or self-doubt. For Sarah, the thought of starting a new painting was overwhelming. What if it didn't turn out as she envisioned? What if others didn't like it? These fears made the act of beginning seem daunting, so she avoided it altogether.

Self-doubt is the lack of confidence in one's abilities. It's the internal critic that questions your worth and undermines your achievements. For Sarah, self-doubt was a constant companion. Despite her undeniable talent, she often questioned her artistic choices and worried that her work wasn't good enough. This persistent self-criticism eroded her confidence and made it difficult for her to trust her creative instincts.

Self-doubt can stem from various sources, including past experiences, societal pressures, and internalized criticism. Sarah's self-doubt was partly fuelled by her perfectionism. She held herself to impossibly high standards and feared that anything less than perfect would be seen as a failure. This fear of not measuring up led to a cycle of self-criticism and avoidance, further entrenching her procrastination.

Procrastination and self-doubt can have a profound impact on creativity and productivity. They create a mental barrier that prevents individuals from fully engaging with their work and expressing their ideas. For Sarah, these silent saboteurs not only hindered her ability to create but also robbed her of the joy and satisfaction that came from painting. The blank canvas became a symbol of her struggles, a reminder of the gap between her potential and her reality.

These forces can be particularly detrimental for individuals in creative fields, where the process of creation is deeply personal and often vulnerable. The fear of judgment and the pressure to produce high-quality work can amplify feelings of procrastination and self-doubt. As a result, many talented individuals like Sarah find themselves stuck in a cycle of inaction and self-criticism, unable to move forward with their creative endeavours.

Understanding the nature of procrastination and self-doubt is the first step towards overcoming them. By recognizing these behaviours and their underlying causes, individuals can begin to develop strategies to manage and mitigate their impact. For Sarah, this journey began with self-awareness. She started by acknowledging her procrastination and self-doubt, recognizing them as obstacles that she needed to address.

One effective strategy for combating procrastination is to break tasks into smaller, more manageable steps. For Sarah, this meant setting specific, achievable goals for each painting session rather than focusing on completing an entire piece. By taking small, incremental steps, she was able to reduce the overwhelm and make progress towards her larger goal.

Building confidence is also crucial in overcoming self-doubt. Sarah began to challenge her negative self-talk and replace it with positive affirmations. She reminded herself of her past successes and the praise she had received for her work. By focusing on her strengths and achievements, she gradually built a more positive self-image and developed greater confidence in her abilities.

Sarah's story is a testament to the power of perseverance and self-awareness in overcoming procrastination and self-doubt. While these silent saboteurs can be formidable, they are not insurmountable. With the right strategies and mindset, it is possible to break free from their grip and unlock one's full potential.

In the chapters that follow, we will explore various techniques and approaches for managing procrastination and self-doubt. From setting clear and achievable goals to building a supportive environment, we will provide practical tools and insights to help you take control of your actions and build confidence in your abilities. By understanding and addressing these silent saboteurs, you can embark on a path of personal and creative growth, achieving the success and fulfilment you deserve.

To delve deeper into the intricacies of procrastination, it's essential to dispel the common misconception that it is merely a result of laziness or poor time management.

Procrastination is often a complex, multi-faceted issue rooted in emotional and psychological factors.

For Sarah, procrastination wasn't about a lack of desire to paint. On the contrary, she deeply wanted to create and share her art. However, the emotional weight of potential failure and criticism created a mental block that was hard to overcome. This block often leads to what is known as "task aversion," where the mind diverts attention to less daunting, often trivial tasks to avoid the discomfort associated with the primary task.

Research in psychology has shown that procrastination is linked to the brain's struggle between the limbic system and the prefrontal cortex. The limbic system, often referred to as the brain's emotional centre, seeks immediate gratification and comfort, driving one to avoid tasks that are perceived as stressful or challenging. On the other hand, the prefrontal cortex is responsible for decision-making, planning, and impulse control.

When the limbic system overrides the prefrontal cortex, procrastination ensues. This battle between immediate pleasure and long-term rewards can be exhausting, leading individuals like Sarah to repeatedly choose short-term comfort over long-term goals. Understanding this internal conflict is crucial for developing strategies to mitigate procrastination.

The Emotional Toll of Self-Doubt

Self-doubt, similarly, is not just a fleeting feeling of uncertainty; it can be a pervasive and crippling force. For Sarah, self-doubt manifested as a constant internal dialogue questioning her worth and capabilities. This self-criticism was not only mentally draining but also paralyzed her ability to act.

Self-doubt often stems from various sources, including past experiences of failure, negative feedback, and societal pressures to meet certain standards. For many, these experiences become internalized, creating a persistent inner critic that undermines confidence and fuels procrastination.

A significant contributor to both procrastination and self-doubt is perfectionism. Perfectionists like Sarah set incredibly high standards for themselves and fear that anything less than perfect is unacceptable. This fear of not meeting their own or others' expectations can lead to a cycle of procrastination and self-doubt, as they avoid starting or completing tasks out of fear of imperfection.

Perfectionism also reinforces a fixed mindset, where individuals believe their abilities are static and unchangeable. This mindset can make the prospect of failure seem even more daunting, as it is perceived as a reflection of inherent inadequacy rather than a learning opportunity.

To overcome perfectionism, it is important to cultivate a growth mindset—a belief that abilities can be developed through dedication and hard work. Sarah began to shift her perspective by embracing the concept of "progress over perfection." She allowed herself to make mistakes and view them as opportunities for growth rather than as failures.

This shift in mindset was liberating for Sarah. It freed her from the paralyzing grip of perfectionism and enabled her to take more risks in her art. By focusing on the process rather than the outcome, she found joy in her creative journey and began to produce more work with greater confidence.

Armed with a better understanding of procrastination and self-doubt, Sarah began to implement practical strategies to combat these challenges. One effective technique was the Pomodoro Technique, which involves working in focused intervals, typically 25 minutes, followed by a short break. This method helped Sarah break her work into manageable chunks and maintain her focus.

Another strategy was to create a structured daily routine. By allocating specific times for her creative work, Sarah established a sense of discipline and consistency. She also made a habit of prioritizing her tasks each day, starting with the most challenging ones when her energy and focus were highest.

Building a Supportive Environment

A supportive environment is crucial for overcoming procrastination and self-doubt. Sarah surrounded herself with positive influences, including fellow artists, mentors, and friends who encouraged and inspired her. She joined an art community where she could share her work and receive constructive feedback, helping to build her confidence and motivation.

Creating a physical space conducive to productivity was also important. Sarah organized her studio to minimize distractions and ensure she had all the tools she needed readily available. A clutter-free, inspiring workspace helped her stay focused and motivated.

Sarah's journey towards overcoming procrastination and self-doubt was also a journey of self-awareness. She began to regularly reflect on her thoughts and behaviours, identifying patterns and triggers that led to procrastination.

This self-awareness allowed her to develop more effective strategies for managing her time and emotions.

Mindfulness practices, such as meditation and journaling, played a significant role in this process. By taking time each day to quiet her mind and reflect on her experiences, Sarah developed a deeper understanding of herself and her motivations. This self-awareness became a powerful tool in her journey towards greater productivity and confidence.

Sarah's story is one of transformation and resilience. By recognizing the silent saboteurs of procrastination and self-doubt and taking proactive steps to address them, she was able to unlock her full potential as an artist. Her journey serves as a reminder that these challenges, while formidable, are not insurmountable.

As we continue through this book, we will explore additional techniques and insights to help you overcome procrastination and self-doubt. By building on the foundation of self-awareness and practical strategies introduced in this chapter, you can embark on your own journey of personal and creative growth, achieving the success and fulfilment you deserve.

Some Final Reflections

Procrastination and self-doubt are powerful forces that can hinder even the most talented individuals. Through the story of Sarah, we have seen how these silent saboteurs can manifest and the impact they can have on creativity and productivity. By understanding their root causes and implementing practical strategies, it is possible to break free from their grip and unlock one's full potential.

Next, we will delve into the importance of setting clear and achievable goals. By learning how to define and pursue your objectives effectively, you can take the next step towards building confidence and overcoming procrastination. The journey towards greater productivity and self-assurance continues, and with each step, you move closer to realizing your true potential.

2: *The Roots of Procrastination*

James had always been seen as the golden boy of his family, excelling in academics and landing a prestigious job straight out of college. With a promising career ahead of him, it seemed like nothing could stand in his way. However, beneath the surface of his apparent success, James struggled with a problem that many of us can relate to procrastination. His habit of putting off important tasks began to take a toll on his professional life, causing his once-bright career to stagnate.

James's story is not unique. Procrastination is a common issue that affects countless individuals, often stemming from deep-rooted psychological triggers. For James, the roots of his procrastination lay in a combination of fear of failure, perfectionism, and feelings of overwhelm. These factors created a perfect storm, making it difficult for him to take decisive action and move forward with his projects.

Fear of failure is a powerful motivator, or rather, a powerful demotivator. For James, the thought of failing at a task was paralyzing. He worried that any mistake would reflect poorly on his abilities and tarnish his reputation. This fear led him to avoid starting tasks altogether, as it seemed safer to delay than to risk failure. The irony, of course, is that by not starting, he was setting himself up for the very failure he feared.

Perfectionism also played a significant role in James's procrastination. He held himself to impossibly high standards, believing that anything less than perfect was unacceptable. This mindset created immense pressure, making even the smallest task feel daunting. The need for perfection paralyzed him, as he feared that his work would never measure up to his expectations. As a result, he often found himself stuck, unable to begin because he couldn't guarantee a flawless outcome.

Feelings of overwhelm further compounded James's struggle. His to-do list seemed endless, and the sheer volume of tasks made it difficult to know where to start. Each task felt like a mountain to climb, and the cumulative weight of them all was crushing. This sense of overwhelm led to a kind of paralysis, where the magnitude of the tasks made it easier to avoid them altogether.

The psychological roots of procrastination are deeply embedded in our brains. To understand this better, we need to delve into the science behind procrastination, particularly the roles of the prefrontal cortex and the limbic system. The prefrontal cortex is the part of our brain responsible for decision-making, planning, and impulse control. It's what allows us to think ahead, set goals, and work towards them.

On the other hand, the limbic system is often referred to as the brain's reward centre. It's responsible for our immediate reactions and the pursuit of pleasure. The limbic system seeks instant gratification and comfort, driving us to engage in activities that feel good in the moment, even if they aren't beneficial in the long run. This system is more primitive, governing our emotions and desires.

In the case of procrastination, there's a constant tug-of-war between the prefrontal cortex and the limbic system. When the limbic system overrides the prefrontal cortex, we choose immediate comfort over long-term benefits. This is why, despite knowing the importance of completing a task, we might find ourselves scrolling through social media or binge-watching a TV show instead.

James's brain was constantly battling between these two systems. His prefrontal cortex understood the importance of his work and the consequences of not completing it on time. However, his limbic system sought to avoid the discomfort associated with starting a difficult task, leading him to engage in more pleasurable, immediate activities.

This internal conflict is something many of us experience daily. We know what we should be doing, but the allure of something easier and more enjoyable often wins out. The immediate reward of relaxation or entertainment can overshadow the long-term benefits of productivity and accomplishment.

Overcoming procrastination involves understanding this internal battle and finding ways to tip the scales in favor of the prefrontal cortex. For James, this meant developing strategies to manage his fear of failure, perfectionism, and feelings of overwhelm. One approach he found helpful was breaking tasks into smaller, more manageable steps. Instead of focusing on the enormity of a project, he concentrated on completing one small part at a time. This made the tasks feel less daunting and allowed him to make steady progress.

Another technique James used was setting specific, achievable goals. Rather than aiming for perfection, he focused on doing his best within a set timeframe. This helped to reduce the pressure he placed on himself and allowed him to start tasks without the fear of not measuring up. By redefining success as progress rather than perfection, he was able to move forward more confidently.

James also learned to manage his feelings of overwhelm by prioritizing his tasks. He made a habit of identifying the most important tasks each day and tackling them first. This not only ensured that he made progress on his most critical projects but also gave him a sense of accomplishment that motivated him to continue.

Another key aspect of overcoming procrastination for James was creating a supportive environment. He found that working in a clutter-free, organized space helped him stay focused and productive. He also sought support from colleagues and mentors who encouraged him and held him accountable for his progress. This support network provided the encouragement and motivation he needed to keep moving forward.

Understanding the psychological roots of procrastination and the internal battle between the prefrontal cortex and the limbic system is crucial for developing effective strategies to overcome it. By addressing the underlying triggers, such as fear of failure, perfectionism, and feelings of overwhelm, and implementing practical techniques to manage them, it's possible to break free from the cycle of procrastination and achieve greater productivity and fulfilment.

James's journey serves as a reminder that procrastination is not a sign of laziness or lack of willpower. It's a complex behaviour rooted in our brain's wiring and influenced by various psychological factors. By approaching it with empathy and understanding, we can develop strategies to manage it and take control of our actions.

In the next chapter, we will explore the concept of self-doubt and its impact on our ability to take action. Through the story of Lisa, we will uncover the origins of self-doubt and provide insights into how to build confidence and trust in our abilities. By addressing both procrastination and self-doubt, we can create a solid foundation for personal and professional growth, enabling us to reach our full potential.

As we move forward, remember that overcoming procrastination is a journey, not a destination. It requires patience, persistence, and self-compassion. By understanding the psychological roots of procrastination and implementing strategies to manage it, you can take the first step towards breaking free from the cycle of delay and inaction.

Embrace the journey, and with each small step, you will move closer to achieving your goals and realizing your dreams.

3: The Anatomy of Self-Doubt

Lisa sat at her desk, her fingers hovering over the keyboard. Her latest story was almost complete, but she hesitated to write the final paragraph. The room was filled with the soft glow of her desk lamp, casting shadows on the pages of her notebook and the stack of books she had read for inspiration. Despite her passion for writing and the hours she had dedicated to perfecting her craft, a persistent voice in her mind whispered doubts. What if her story wasn't good enough? What if readers didn't connect with her characters or understand her themes? The fear of judgment and failure kept her from finishing, let alone sharing her work.

Self-doubt is a powerful force, one that can paralyze even the most talented and dedicated individuals. For Lisa, self-doubt was like an unwelcome companion, always present, always critical. Her journey as a writer had been fraught with moments of hesitation and insecurity, despite the praise she had received from friends and mentors. To understand the anatomy of self-doubt, we must delve into its origins and explore how it impacts our decisions and confidence.

The roots of self-doubt often lie in our childhood experiences. For Lisa, the seeds of doubt were planted early. She grew up in a family where academic achievement was highly valued, and there was little room for failure. Mistakes were met with disappointment, and success was expected. This environment fostered a fear of not measuring up and a constant need for validation. Lisa learned to equate her worth with her accomplishments, and any perceived failure felt like a personal shortcoming.

Societal pressures further compounded Lisa's self-doubt. As she navigated through school and into adulthood, the expectations placed upon her only grew. Society has a way of setting standards that can feel impossible to meet, especially for those in creative fields. Writers like Lisa are often expected to produce work that is not only technically proficient but also original and thought-provoking. The pressure to meet these high standards can be overwhelming, leading to a constant fear of falling short.

Internalized criticism is another significant contributor to self-doubt. Over the years, Lisa had internalized the critical voices of teachers, peers, and even herself. Whenever she sat down to write, these voices echoed in her mind, questioning her choices and undermining her confidence. This internal critic was relentless, magnifying every flaw and dismissing any praise. It made her question her abilities and second-guess her creative instincts.

The psychological impact of self-doubt is profound. It affects not only our confidence but also our decision-making processes. For Lisa, self-doubt manifested as a constant state of indecision. She would spend hours rewriting the same paragraph, never feeling satisfied with her work. This perfectionism was driven by the fear that her writing would never be good enough. It led to procrastination, as starting a new project felt daunting when she wasn't sure she could meet her own high standards.

Self-doubt also creates a sense of vulnerability that can be difficult to overcome. Sharing one's work, especially something as personal as writing, requires a level of openness and courage. For Lisa, the thought of exposing her innermost thoughts and feelings to others was terrifying. She feared that her work would be judged harshly, and that this judgment would confirm her deepest insecurities. This fear kept her from submitting her stories to publishers and sharing them with a wider audience.

Understanding the origins and effects of self-doubt is the first step towards overcoming it. For Lisa, this meant acknowledging the critical voices and recognizing their impact on her confidence and creativity. It was a difficult process, but one that was necessary for her growth as a writer and as a person.

One of the most effective ways Lisa began to address her self-doubt was through self-compassion. She learned to treat herself with the same kindness and understanding that she would offer a friend. This involved recognizing that everyone makes mistakes, and that imperfection is a natural part of the creative process. By giving herself permission to be imperfect, she was able to reduce the pressure she placed on herself and approach her work with a more open and positive mindset.

Another important strategy was challenging the negative self-talk. Lisa began to identify the critical voices and counter them with positive affirmations. When the internal critic questioned her abilities, she reminded herself of her achievements and the positive feedback she had received. This helped to build her confidence and create a more balanced perspective.

Lisa also found it helpful to set realistic goals and celebrate small successes. Rather than aiming for perfection, she focused on making steady progress and acknowledging her efforts. This approach made the writing process more enjoyable and less stressful, allowing her to take pride in her work regardless of the outcome.

Seeking support from others was another crucial step in overcoming self-doubt. Lisa joined a writers' group where she could share her work and receive constructive feedback. This supportive environment provided validation and encouragement, helping to bolster her confidence. The group also offered a sense of community, reminding her that she was not alone in her struggles.

Mindfulness and self-reflection played a significant role in Lisa's journey. By taking time each day to reflect on her thoughts and feelings, she gained a deeper understanding of her self-doubt and its triggers. Mindfulness practices, such as meditation and journaling, allowed her to quiet the critical voices and focus on the present moment. This helped to reduce anxiety and create a sense of calm and clarity.

Through these strategies, Lisa gradually began to overcome her self-doubt and embrace her creative potential. She learned that self-doubt is a natural part of the human experience and that it doesn't have to define her. By addressing the underlying causes and developing a more compassionate and balanced perspective, she was able to reclaim her confidence and move forward with her writing.

The story of Lisa's struggle with self-doubt is a powerful reminder of the challenges that many of us face. Whether we are writers, artists, or professionals in any field, self-doubt can hold us back and prevent us from realizing our full potential. However, by understanding its origins and impact, and by developing strategies to address it, we can learn to navigate these doubts and build the confidence we need to succeed.

As we continue our journey, remember that overcoming self-doubt is not a one-time event but an ongoing process. It requires patience, persistence, and self-compassion. By embracing our imperfections and focusing on progress rather than perfection, we can create a more positive and empowering narrative for ourselves. And with each step we take, we move closer to achieving our dreams and realizing our true potential.

In the next section, we will explore the vicious cycle between procrastination and self-doubt. Through the story of Tom, we will see how these two forces can reinforce each other, creating a loop that can be difficult to break. By understanding this cycle and implementing strategies to disrupt it, we can take control of our actions and build a more productive and fulfilling life.

4: The Vicious Cycle

Meet Tom, a bright and ambitious entrepreneur with a groundbreaking idea for a startup. Tom had everything he needed to succeed: a solid business plan, financial backing, and a supportive network. Yet, despite these advantages, he found himself unable to launch his business. Day after day, he would sit at his desk, staring at his computer screen, unable to take the necessary steps to move forward. His problem wasn't a lack of resources or knowledge; it was the paralyzing cycle of procrastination and self-doubt.

Understanding the Cycle

Tom's story is a poignant example of how procrastination and self-doubt can feed off each other, creating a vicious cycle that is difficult to break. At its core, procrastination is a coping mechanism that helps us avoid the discomfort of facing challenging tasks. For Tom, the fear of failure and the immense pressure to succeed made starting his business seem daunting. Each time he put off an important task, he felt a temporary sense of relief. However, this relief was short-lived and often followed by feelings of guilt and inadequacy.

These feelings of inadequacy fuelled Tom's self-doubt. He began to question his abilities and wonder if he was truly capable of turning his vision into reality. This self-doubt made him even more reluctant to act, leading to further procrastination. And so, the cycle continued, each turn of the wheel reinforcing his belief that he wasn't good enough.

The Psychology Behind the Cycle

To understand why this cycle is so powerful, we need to look at the psychology behind procrastination and self-doubt. Procrastination is often driven by a desire to avoid negative emotions such as fear, anxiety, and self-criticism. When faced with a task that we perceive as difficult or threatening, our brain seeks to protect us by diverting our attention to more pleasant activities. This avoidance behaviour provides immediate, albeit temporary, relief from the discomfort.

However, avoiding the task doesn't make the problem go away. Instead, it creates additional stress and compounds the negative feelings we were trying to escape. As deadlines approach and the pressure mounts, we feel increasingly overwhelmed and incapable of handling the task. This heightened stress and self-criticism lead to more procrastination, creating a self-perpetuating cycle.

Self-doubt plays a crucial role in this cycle. When we doubt our abilities, we are less likely to take risks and more likely to avoid challenges. Tom's fear of failure was a significant source of his self-doubt. He worried that if his startup didn't succeed, it would confirm his worst fears about his inadequacy. This fear made him hesitant to take action, reinforcing his procrastination.

Real-Life Impact

The impact of this vicious cycle can be devastating, not only for our professional lives but also for our mental and emotional well-being. For Tom, the cycle of procrastination and self-doubt led to missed opportunities and stalled progress. The longer he delayed launching his startup, the more his confidence eroded. He began to feel like a failure, not because of any inherent lack of ability, but because he couldn't break free from the cycle.

Tom's experience is not unique. Many talented and capable individuals find themselves trapped in this destructive loop. The longer the cycle continues, the harder it becomes to break out of it. The constant self-criticism and fear of failure create a mindset that is resistant to change. This can lead to chronic procrastination, where even small tasks feel insurmountable.

While the cycle of procrastination and self-doubt can be deeply entrenched, it is possible to break free. The first step is to recognize and acknowledge the cycle. Understanding that procrastination is a coping mechanism, and that self-doubt is a natural response to fear can help to reduce the shame and guilt associated with these behaviours.

One effective strategy for breaking the cycle is to set small, manageable goals. For Tom, this meant breaking down the process of launching his startup into smaller, actionable steps. Instead of focusing on the overwhelming task of starting a business, he set specific, achievable goals for each day. This approach made the process feel less daunting and provided a sense of accomplishment with each completed task.

Another important strategy is to challenge negative self-talk. Tom began to recognize the critical voice in his head and question its validity. He reminded himself of his past successes and the positive feedback he had received. By reframing his thoughts and focusing on his strengths, he was able to build a more balanced and realistic self-image.

Seeking Support

Support from others can also be incredibly valuable in breaking the cycle of procrastination and self-doubt. Tom reached out to his mentors and peers for advice and encouragement. Sharing his struggles with others helped to normalize his experience and reduce feelings of isolation. His support network provided practical advice and emotional support, helping him to stay motivated and focused.

Creating a structured routine was another key component of Tom's strategy. He established a daily schedule that included time for focused work, breaks, and self-care. This routine helped him to create a sense of order and predictability, reducing the anxiety associated with unstructured time. By prioritizing self-care, Tom was able to manage his stress levels and maintain his energy and motivation.

Mindfulness and Reflection

Mindfulness and self-reflection played a significant role in Tom's journey. By practicing mindfulness, he learned to observe his thoughts and emotions without judgment. This helped him to become more aware of his triggers for procrastination and self-doubt. Through journaling, he reflected on his experiences and identified patterns in his behaviour. This self-awareness allowed him to develop more effective strategies for managing his procrastination.

Tom also made a conscious effort to celebrate his successes, no matter how small. Recognizing and celebrating progress helped to reinforce positive behaviour and build his confidence. Over time, these small victories accumulated, creating a positive momentum that helped him to break free from the cycle.

Breaking the cycle of procrastination and self-doubt is not an overnight process. It requires patience, persistence, and self-compassion. For Tom, it was a journey of self-discovery and growth. By understanding the psychological roots of his procrastination and addressing his self-doubt, he was able to take meaningful steps towards launching his startup.

Tom's story is a powerful reminder that we all have the capacity to overcome our internal barriers. While the cycle of procrastination and self-doubt can be challenging, it is not insurmountable. With the right strategies and support, we can break free from this cycle and achieve our goals.

5: Strategies to Begin Breaking Free

As we move forward, it's important to keep in mind some initial strategies to help break the cycle of procrastination and self-doubt:

1. Set Small, Achievable Goals: Break down larger tasks into smaller, manageable steps. Focus on completing one step at a time to reduce overwhelm and build momentum.

2. Challenge Negative Self-Talk: Recognize and question the critical voice in your head. Replace negative thoughts

with positive affirmations and reminders of your strengths and achievements.

3. Seek Support: Reach out to friends, family, mentors, or support groups. Sharing your struggles can provide validation and encouragement, and others may offer valuable insights and advice.

4. Create a Structured Routine: Establish a daily schedule that includes time for focused work, breaks, and self-care. A structured routine can reduce anxiety and create a sense of order and predictability.

5. Practice Mindfulness and Self-Reflection: Use mindfulness techniques to observe your thoughts and emotions without judgment. Reflect on your experiences to identify patterns and develop more effective strategies for managing procrastination.

6. Celebrate Progress: Recognize and celebrate your successes, no matter how small. Celebrating progress reinforces positive behaviour and builds confidence.

Breaking the cycle of procrastination and self-doubt is a journey. It's important to be patient with yourself and to approach this process with kindness and self-compassion.

Each step you take towards understanding and addressing these behaviours is a step towards greater self-awareness, productivity, and fulfilment.

6: Breaking Down the Barriers

Maria always had a passion for baking. From a young age, she found solace in her kitchen, experimenting with recipes and creating delicious treats for her family and friends. Her dream was to one day open her own bakery, a cozy little place where people could come to enjoy her creations and feel at home. However, like many of us, Maria found herself trapped in a cycle of procrastination and self-doubt. The idea of turning her passion into a business seemed daunting, and she was overwhelmed by the thought of everything that could go wrong.

Maria's story is one of transformation, a journey from hesitation to action, and it offers valuable insights into how we can break down the barriers that hold us back. One of the first steps Maria took was to set small, achievable goals. The prospect of opening a bakery felt enormous but breaking it down into manageable tasks made it seem more attainable. She started by researching the basics of running a business, reading articles, and talking to local bakery owners. Each small step she took built her confidence and moved her closer to her goal.

Setting small, achievable goals is a powerful way to combat procrastination. When a task feels too big, it's easy to become paralyzed by the enormity of it. By breaking it down into smaller parts, we can make steady progress without feeling overwhelmed. For Maria, this meant focusing on one aspect of her business at a time. One week, she would work on her business plan; the next, she would look into finding a location. Each small accomplishment gave her a sense of achievement and motivated her to keep going.

Developing a positive mindset was another crucial element in Maria's journey. Self-doubt often stems from negative self-talk and a lack of confidence in our abilities. Maria found herself constantly questioning her skills and worrying about failure. To counteract this, she began practicing positive affirmations. Every morning, she would spend a few minutes reminding herself of her strengths and the progress she had made. She kept a journal where she noted down her achievements, no matter how small, and reflected on them whenever she felt discouraged.

Positive affirmations and self-reflection can help rewire our thinking patterns. By focusing on our strengths and accomplishments, we can gradually shift our mindset from one of doubt to one of confidence. Maria's journal became a source of encouragement, a tangible reminder of her capabilities and the progress she had made. This practice helped her to build resilience and maintain a positive outlook, even when faced with challenges.

Employing cognitive-behavioural techniques was another strategy that proved effective for Maria. Cognitive-behavioural therapy (CBT) is a well-established method for addressing negative thought patterns and behaviours. Maria learned to identify the negative thoughts that were holding her back and challenge them. For example, when she found herself thinking, "I'm not good enough to run a business," she would counter this thought with evidence of her skills and past successes. By questioning the validity of her negative thoughts, she was able to reduce their power over her.

CBT techniques can be incredibly helpful in breaking down the barriers of procrastination and self-doubt. By becoming aware of our negative thoughts and actively challenging them, we can change the way we perceive ourselves and our abilities. For Maria, this process involved a lot of self-reflection and honesty. She had to confront her fears and insecurities, but by doing so, she was able to gain a clearer perspective and build a stronger sense of self-belief.

Maria also found that creating a supportive environment was key to her success. She surrounded herself with positive influences, including friends, family, and mentors who encouraged and believed in her. Sharing her goals and progress with others provided accountability and motivation. Her friends would check in on her progress, offer advice, and celebrate her achievements. This network of support helped Maria stay focused and motivated, especially during difficult times.

Having a supportive environment can make a significant difference in our ability to overcome procrastination and self-doubt. Surrounding ourselves with positive, encouraging people provides us with the emotional and practical support we need to keep moving forward. For Maria, her support network was a source of strength and inspiration, reminding her that she was not alone in her journey.

Another strategy Maria employed was to embrace the concept of "progress over perfection." Perfectionism is a common barrier to taking action, as it creates unrealistic standards that can be paralyzing. Maria learned to let go of the need for everything to be perfect and instead focused on making steady progress. She reminded herself that it was okay to make mistakes and that each misstep was an opportunity to learn and grow.

Adopting a mindset of progress over perfection allows us to take risks and move forward without the fear of failure. For Maria, this meant being kinder to herself and accepting that her journey would have ups and downs. By focusing on progress rather than perfection, she was able to keep moving forward and avoid getting stuck in a cycle of self-criticism.

Maria also made a conscious effort to celebrate her successes, no matter how small. Recognizing and celebrating progress is important for maintaining motivation and building confidence. Each time Maria reached a milestone, she took the time to acknowledge her achievement and reward herself. Whether it was treating herself to a nice dinner or simply taking a moment to reflect on her progress, these celebrations helped her to stay motivated and focused on her goals.

Celebrating our successes helps to reinforce positive behaviour and build momentum. It provides us with the encouragement we need to keep going, even when the road ahead seems challenging. For Maria, these celebrations were a way to honour her hard work and remind herself of how far she had come.

As Maria continued to break down the barriers of procrastination and self-doubt, she found herself gaining confidence and making tangible progress towards her dream. Her journey was not without its challenges, but each step she took brought her closer to her goal. By setting small, achievable goals, developing a positive mindset, employing cognitive-behavioural techniques, creating a supportive environment, embracing progress over perfection, and celebrating her successes, Maria was able to overcome her fears and start a successful business.

Maria's story is a testament to the power of persistence and self-belief. Breaking down the barriers of procrastination and self-doubt is not an easy task, but with the right strategies and support, it is possible to overcome these obstacles and achieve our goals. Her journey serves as a reminder that we all have the capacity to overcome our internal barriers and create a fulfilling and successful life.

As we continue our own journeys, it is important to remember that breaking down these barriers is an ongoing process. It requires patience, self-compassion, and a willingness to keep moving forward, even when the path ahead seems uncertain. By implementing the strategies that worked for Maria, we can start making tangible progress, building confidence with each step, and ultimately achieve our dreams.

7: The Power of Self-Awareness

Alex had always been a man of dreams and ambitions. He wanted to achieve great things in life, but there was something always holding him back. Despite his best efforts, he found himself stuck in a loop of procrastination and self-doubt. His days were filled with the nagging feeling that he wasn't living up to his potential. The weight of unfulfilled goals and unfinished tasks hung heavy over him, clouding his mind and dampening his spirit.

One day, Alex decided he had had enough. He realized that if he wanted to break free from this cycle, he needed to understand what was truly holding him back. This realization marked the beginning of a profound journey of self-awareness that would eventually transform his life.

The first step in Alex's journey was to acknowledge his feelings of procrastination and self-doubt without judgment. He began to pay attention to his thoughts and emotions, noticing how they influenced his actions. Instead of berating himself for not being productive, he started to explore why he felt the way he did. This gentle curiosity was a significant shift from his usual pattern of self-criticism.

Alex discovered that much of his procrastination stemmed from a fear of failure. The tasks he put off were often the ones that mattered most to him, the ones where the stakes felt highest. This fear paralyzed him, making it easier to avoid the task altogether than to face the possibility of not meeting his own expectations. By acknowledging this fear, Alex took the first step towards addressing it.

He also noticed that his self-doubt was deeply rooted in his past experiences. Growing up, Alex had been surrounded by high achievers, and he often felt like he couldn't measure up. This comparison had ingrained a sense of inadequacy in him, making him doubt his capabilities. Recognizing this helped Alex understand that his self-doubt wasn't a reflection of his actual abilities but rather a learned behaviour.

To delve deeper into his thought patterns, Alex began journaling. Every morning, he would spend a few minutes writing about his thoughts, feelings, and experiences. This practice allowed him to externalize his internal dialogue and see it from a different perspective. Through journaling, Alex identified recurring themes and triggers that fuelled his procrastination and self-doubt.

For instance, he realized that he often procrastinated on tasks that required creative thinking. The pressure to produce something original and impressive overwhelmed him, leading to avoidance. By writing about these experiences, Alex could dissect them and understand their roots. This self-awareness was liberating; it gave him a sense of control over his actions.

Meditation became another crucial tool in Alex's journey. He started with just a few minutes each day, focusing on his breath and observing his thoughts without attachment. This practice helped him cultivate mindfulness, a state of being present and aware of the moment. Through meditation, Alex learned to detach from his negative thoughts and see them as transient rather than defining.

Mindfulness also allowed Alex to recognize the physical sensations associated with his procrastination and self-doubt. He noticed that when he felt anxious about a task, his shoulders tensed, and his breath became shallow. By tuning into these bodily signals, he could catch himself before the anxiety spiralled into avoidance. This awareness empowered him to take proactive steps to calm his mind and body, such as deep breathing or a short walk.

Self-assessment exercises further enhanced Alex's self-awareness. He regularly took time to reflect on his strengths, weaknesses, and areas for growth. This practice was not about self-criticism but about gaining a balanced view of himself. Alex realized that while he had areas to improve, he also had many strengths that he often overlooked. Acknowledging these strengths boosted his confidence and motivated him to act.

One of the most transformative insights Alex gained was the understanding that his self-worth was not tied to his achievements. For a long time, he had believed that he needed to accomplish certain things to prove his value. This belief had driven much of his anxiety and procrastination. Through self-reflection, Alex began to separate his sense of self from his accomplishments. He learned to appreciate himself for who he was, not just for what he did.

As Alex's self-awareness grew, so did his ability to combat procrastination and self-doubt. He started setting realistic goals and breaking them down into manageable steps. Instead of focusing on the daunting end result, he concentrated on the process, taking one small step at a time. This approach reduced his overwhelm and made it easier to start tasks.

He also developed a more compassionate inner dialogue. When he noticed self-doubt creeping in, he countered it with positive affirmations. Instead of telling himself, "I can't do this," he reminded himself of past successes and said, "I've overcome challenges before, and I can do it again." This shift in mindset was empowering and helped him build resilience.

Alex's journey wasn't without setbacks. There were days when procrastination and self-doubt reared their heads, but he no longer let them derail him. With his newfound self-awareness, he could recognize these moments for what they were—temporary lapses rather than defining traits. This perspective allowed him to bounce back more quickly and stay on track.

One of the most profound changes Alex experienced was a deeper connection with himself. Through mindfulness and self-reflection, he developed a greater understanding of his desires, motivations, and values. This self-knowledge guided his decisions and actions, aligning them more closely with his true self. As a result, he felt more fulfilled and at peace with his choices.

Alex's story is a testament to the transformative power of self-awareness. By taking the time to understand his thoughts, emotions, and behaviours, he was able to break free from the cycle of procrastination and self-doubt. His journey shows that self-awareness is not just a tool for personal growth but a foundation for meaningful change.

The tools Alex used—journaling, meditation, and self-assessment exercises—are accessible to anyone willing to embark on a similar journey. Journaling allows us to externalize our internal dialogue and gain a clearer perspective on our thoughts and emotions. It helps us identify patterns and triggers, providing valuable insights into our behaviour.

Meditation cultivates mindfulness, enabling us to observe our thoughts without judgment and detach from negative thought patterns. It enhances our ability to stay present and calm, reducing the impact of anxiety and self-doubt. Through meditation, we learn to recognize our physical and emotional responses, empowering us to take proactive steps to manage them.

Self-assessment exercises provide a balanced view of ourselves, highlighting both our strengths and areas for growth. They encourage us to reflect on our values, motivations, and goals, helping us align our actions with our true selves. This practice fosters self-compassion and resilience, enabling us to navigate challenges with confidence.

As we embrace these tools and practices, we cultivate a deeper understanding of ourselves. This self-awareness is the foundation for overcoming procrastination and self-doubt. It allows us to recognize the internal barriers that hold us back and develop strategies to break them down. By gaining insights into our thought patterns and behaviours, we can make meaningful changes that lead to personal growth and fulfilment.

Alex's journey reminds us that self-awareness is a lifelong process. It requires patience, curiosity, and a willingness to explore our inner world. But the rewards are profound—a greater sense of control over our lives, a deeper connection with ourselves, and the ability to achieve our goals with confidence.

As you continue on your own journey, remember that self-awareness is the key to unlocking your potential. Take the time to reflect, meditate, and assess yourself regularly. Embrace your strengths and acknowledge your areas for growth with compassion. By doing so, you will build a solid foundation for overcoming procrastination and self-doubt and create a life that aligns with your true self.

In the next section, we will explore practical strategies for sustaining long-term success. Through the story of Claire, we will learn how to maintain the momentum of personal growth and navigate the challenges that come with it.

Together, we will continue to build on the foundation of self-awareness and create a path towards lasting fulfilment and achievement.

8: *The First Step Towards Change*

Claire had always been a dreamer. She had a vision of herself leading a fulfilled life, achieving her goals, and making a difference in the world. But for years, her dreams remained just that—dreams. Every time she tried to take a step forward, she was held back by the familiar enemies of procrastination and self-doubt. The weight of her unfulfilled potential pressed heavily on her, and she often wondered if she would ever break free from the cycle that kept her stuck.

One particularly challenging day, after feeling overwhelmed and disheartened by yet another unproductive week, Claire had a moment of clarity. She realized that if she wanted to change her life, she had to confront her procrastination and self-doubt head-on. This realization was both terrifying and liberating. For the first time, she acknowledged that the power to change lay within her. This was the beginning of Claire's journey towards transformation.

Claire's first step was to admit that she had been avoiding tasks because they felt too daunting. She often put off starting projects, convincing herself that she needed more time to prepare or that the timing wasn't right. Deep down, she knew that these were just excuses born out of fear. Admitting this to herself was difficult, but it was a crucial step. It was only by acknowledging her fears that she could begin to address them.

Determined to make a change, Claire decided to start small. She set a goal to spend just ten minutes each day working on a task she had been avoiding. At first, even this seemed challenging, but she reminded herself that ten minutes was better than nothing. Each time she completed her ten-minute task, she felt a sense of accomplishment. Gradually, those ten minutes turned into twenty, and then thirty. By breaking her tasks into manageable chunks, she was able to make steady progress without feeling overwhelmed.

As Claire began to see progress, her confidence grew. She started to challenge the negative thoughts that had held her back for so long. Whenever she felt the familiar pangs of self-doubt, she reminded herself of her small victories. She kept a journal where she documented her daily accomplishments, no matter how minor they seemed. This practice helped her to focus on her progress rather than her perceived shortcomings.

One of the most powerful realizations Claire had was that her worth was not defined by her achievements. For years, she had equated her value with her productivity, believing that she needed to accomplish great things to prove her worth. This belief had fuelled her procrastination and self-doubt, creating a vicious cycle that was hard to break. By reflecting on her experiences, Claire began to see that her worth was inherent. She didn't need to earn it through accomplishments.

This shift in perspective was transformative. It allowed Claire to approach her tasks with a sense of curiosity and enjoyment rather than fear and pressure. She began to see challenges as opportunities for growth rather than threats to her self-worth. This new mindset made it easier for her to take risks and embrace the learning process, even when it involved mistakes and setbacks.

As Claire continued to confront her procrastination and self-doubt, she also made a conscious effort to practice self-compassion. She realized that she had been her harshest critic, constantly berating herself for not doing enough. This self-criticism only added to her stress and made it harder for her to take action. By treating herself with kindness and understanding, she was able to create a more supportive inner environment.

Self-compassion became a cornerstone of Claire's transformation. Instead of punishing herself for procrastinating, she would gently acknowledge her feelings and encourage herself to try again. She began to speak to herself as she would a dear friend, offering words of encouragement and reassurance. This practice helped to build her resilience and maintain her motivation.

Claire's journey was not without its challenges. There were days when she felt stuck and doubted whether she was making any real progress. But each time she encountered a setback, she reminded herself of how far she had come. She reached out to friends and mentors for support, sharing her struggles and celebrating her successes. This sense of community provided her with the strength and encouragement she needed to keep moving forward.

Over time, Claire began to see significant changes in her life. She completed projects that had been lingering for months, and she started new ventures with a sense of excitement and confidence. Her relationships improved as she became more present and engaged, and she felt a renewed sense of purpose and fulfilment. The transformation she experienced was profound, and it all began with the decision to take that first step towards change.

Claire's story is a powerful reminder that change is possible, no matter how deeply entrenched our habits and fears may seem. The first step towards change is often the hardest, but it is also the most important. By confronting our procrastination and self-doubt head-on, we can begin to break free from the cycle that holds us back.

The journey towards change is not about perfection; it is about progress. It is about recognizing our fears and limitations and choosing to move forward despite them. It is about setting small, achievable goals and celebrating each step we take. It is about being kind to ourselves and acknowledging our inherent worth, regardless of our achievements.

As you embark on your own journey towards change, remember that you are not alone. Many have walked this path before you, and their stories serve as a testament to the power of persistence and self-belief. You have within you the strength and resilience to overcome your internal barriers and create the life you envision.

Take a moment to reflect on your own experiences of procrastination and self-doubt. What fears or beliefs have been holding you back? What small step can you take today to begin addressing these challenges? Remember that every journey begins with a single step, and each step you take brings you closer to your goals.

As we move forward, we will delve into setting clear and achievable goals to continue this journey of personal transformation. By defining our objectives and creating a roadmap for success, we can build on the foundation we have established and maintain our momentum. The road ahead may be challenging, but with determination and self-awareness, we can navigate it with confidence and purpose.

The first step towards change is a courageous act of self-awareness and commitment. It is an acknowledgment that we have the power to shape our own destinies and the willingness to act. Claire's story is a testament to the transformative power of this first step, and it serves as an inspiration for us all. As you embark on your own journey, embrace the process, celebrate your progress, and trust in your ability to create meaningful change in your life.

The journey may be long, but the rewards are immeasurable. Take that first step today and see where it leads you.

Chapter 2: Setting Clear and Achievable Goals

"It can be overwhelming to tackle big goals, especially when procrastination and self-doubt are holding you back. From my experience, setting clear, specific, and achievable goals is a game-changer.

In this chapter, will guide you through practical steps to define your objectives, break them down into manageable tasks, and create a detailed roadmap for success. By setting the right goals, you can start building your confidence and making meaningful progress, one step at a time. Let's embark on this journey together and overcome those barriers that have been standing in your way."

Synopsis

Let's continue to overcome procrastination and self-doubt by setting clear and achievable goals. Setting the right goals can make all the difference in building confidence and making consistent progress. This chapter will guide you through the process of defining your objectives, breaking them down into manageable tasks, and creating a practical roadmap for success. Let's embark on this journey together.

1: Understanding the Importance of Clear Goals

Imagine setting off on a journey without a map. You might have a destination in mind, but without clear directions, you're likely to get lost or give up. Setting clear goals is like drawing a map for your journey. It provides you with direction, purpose, and a sense of accomplishment as you reach each milestone. Clear goals help to reduce overwhelm, making it easier to focus on one step at a time rather than feeling lost in the enormity of your aspirations.

2: Defining Your Objectives

To begin, it's essential to clearly define what you want to achieve. This might sound simple, but vague goals can lead to vague results. Instead of saying, "I want to be successful," try to be more specific. Ask yourself what success looks like for you. Is it starting a new business, writing a book, or improving your health? The more specific you are, the easier it will be to create a plan to achieve it.

Take some time to reflect on your long-term aspirations and then break them down into specific objectives. For instance, if your goal is to start a business, your specific objectives might include researching your market, developing a business plan, and securing funding.

3: Breaking Down Goals into Manageable Tasks

Once you have clear objectives, the next step is to break them down into smaller, manageable tasks. This is where the magic happens. Large goals can feel overwhelming and unattainable, but when you break them down into smaller tasks, they become much more manageable.

Think of each task as a stepping stone on your path to success. For example, if one of your objectives is to develop a business plan, break it down into smaller tasks like researching business plans, outlining your plan, and writing each section step-by-step. This approach not only makes the process less daunting but also allows you to celebrate small victories along the way, keeping you motivated and engaged.

4: Creating a Roadmap for Success

Now that you have your objectives and tasks outlined, it's time to create a roadmap. A roadmap is essentially a timeline that outlines when and how you will complete each task. This helps to keep you organized and ensures that you're making steady progress towards your goals.

Start by setting deadlines for each task. Be realistic about the time you have available and the effort each task requires. It's better to set achievable deadlines than to rush and feel overwhelmed. Remember, the goal is to make steady progress, not to complete everything at once.

Use tools that work best for you, whether it's a planner, a digital calendar, or project management software. Regularly review your roadmap to track your progress and adjust as needed. Life can be unpredictable, and it's okay to revise your plan to accommodate changes. The key is to stay flexible and committed to your overall objectives.

5: Overcoming Obstacles and Staying Motivated

As you work towards your goals, it's natural to encounter obstacles and moments of doubt. This is where self-awareness and resilience come into play. When you face challenges, remind yourself of why you set these goals in the first place. Reflect on your motivations and the benefits of achieving your objectives.

Stay connected to your progress by celebrating small achievements. Each task you complete brings you one step closer to your goal. Use these moments to boost your confidence and reinforce your commitment. Share your progress with a supportive friend or mentor who can provide encouragement and accountability.

6: Building Confidence Through Action

Taking consistent action towards your goals is the best way to build confidence. Each step you take, no matter how small, is a testament to your commitment and capability. As you make progress, you'll find that your self-doubt diminishes, and your confidence grows.

The journey towards achieving your goals is just as important as the destination. Embrace the process, learn from setbacks, and celebrate your growth. By setting clear and achievable goals, breaking them down into manageable tasks, and creating a roadmap for success, you're building a solid foundation for personal and professional growth.

7: Take Out

Setting clear, specific, and achievable goals is a powerful strategy for overcoming procrastination and self-doubt. By defining your objectives, breaking them down into manageable tasks, and creating a roadmap for success, you can make consistent progress and build confidence with each step.

The journey is a process, and each small victory is a testament to your dedication and resilience. Let's continue this journey together, one step at a time.

1: Understanding the Importance of Clear Goals

Setting goals is like setting a compass for your journey through life. Without clear goals, it's easy to feel adrift, to lack direction and purpose, and to fall into the traps of procrastination and self-doubt. Understanding the importance of clear goals is the foundation upon which you can build a more structured, confident, and fulfilled life. Let's delve into why clear goals matter so much and how they can transform your approach to achieving what you desire.

Imagine waking up every day without a clear idea of what you want to achieve. You might have vague notions of success, happiness, or accomplishment, but without specific goals, these concepts remain abstract and unattainable. Clear goals turn abstract dreams into concrete targets. They give you something tangible to aim for, which in turn helps to focus your efforts and energy.

When you set clear goals, you're essentially giving yourself a roadmap. Instead of wandering aimlessly, you have a defined path to follow. This path doesn't have to be rigid or unchangeable but having it in place provides structure. It helps you prioritize your actions and make decisions that align with your desired outcomes. Without clear goals, it's easy to get lost in the day-to-day noise and distractions, which can lead to feelings of frustration and stagnation.

One of the primary reasons people struggle with procrastination and self-doubt is the lack of clear goals. When you don't know exactly what you're working towards, it's hard to muster the motivation to get started. Tasks can feel overwhelming and purposeless. On the other hand, when you have a clear goal, every task you undertake has a purpose. You can see how each step contributes to your overall objective, which makes it easier to stay motivated and on track.

Clear goals also play a crucial role in building confidence. Each time you set and achieve a goal, no matter how small, you're proving to yourself that you're capable. This builds a sense of competence and self-efficacy. The more you accomplish, the more confident you become in your abilities. This growing confidence helps to combat self-doubt and encourages you to take on bigger and more challenging goals.

Consider the goal-setting process as a form of self-commitment. When you set a goal, you're making a commitment to yourself. This commitment is a powerful motivator because it taps into your intrinsic desire to follow through on your promises. Breaking down this commitment into smaller, manageable steps further reinforces your determination. Each small step completed is a promise kept to yourself, which strengthens your resolve and boosts your self-esteem.

Set Goals to Take Control

Another significant aspect of clear goal setting is the sense of control it provides. Life can often feel chaotic and unpredictable. Clear goals act as anchors, giving you a sense of direction amidst the uncertainty. They provide a framework that helps you manage your time and resources more effectively. Instead of reacting to circumstances, you can proactively work towards your goals, which enhances your sense of control and reduces anxiety.

Clear goals also foster resilience. The path to achieving your goals is rarely smooth; it's filled with challenges and setbacks. When you have clear goals, you're better equipped to navigate these obstacles. You can maintain focus on your end objective, which helps you stay motivated even when things get tough. Moreover, the clarity of your goals allows you to develop contingency plans and alternative strategies, making you more adaptable and resilient in the face of adversity.

In setting clear goals, it's important to be specific. Vague goals like "I want to be successful" or "I want to be happy" are difficult to achieve because they lack clarity. Specific goals, on the other hand, provide a clear target. For example, "I want to start a business by the end of the year" or "I want to run a marathon in six months" are specific goals that give you a concrete aim. Specificity makes it easier to create a plan of action and measure your progress.

Measurable goals are another critical component of clear goal setting. Being able to track your progress is essential for maintaining motivation and adjusting your strategies as needed. Measurable goals provide a way to quantify your efforts and see tangible results. For instance, if your goal is to improve your fitness, setting a measurable goal like "I will exercise for 30 minutes five times a week" allows you to track your workouts and see your progress over time.

Achievable goals are realistic and attainable. While it's important to challenge yourself, setting goals that are too ambitious can lead to frustration and discouragement. Achievable goals take into account your current abilities and resources. They allow for incremental progress, which builds confidence and keeps you motivated. For example, if you're new to running, setting a goal to run a 5K in three months is achievable and gives you a clear target to work towards.

Relevant goals align with your values and long term aspirations. They are meaningful and significant to you, which provides intrinsic motivation to pursue them. When setting goals, consider why they matter to you. How do they fit into your overall vision for your life? Goals that are relevant and personally meaningful are more likely to keep you engaged and committed.

Time-bound goals have a deadline. They create a sense of urgency and help you prioritize your actions. Without a time frame, goals can easily be postponed indefinitely. Time-bound goals provide a clear timeline for achieving your objectives, which helps you stay focused and accountable.

For example, "I will complete my novel by the end of the year" gives you a specific time frame to work within, which encourages consistent effort and progress.

SMART Goals

The SMART criteria (Specific, Measurable, Achievable, Relevant, Time-bound) is a powerful tool for setting clear goals. By applying these criteria to your goals, you create a detailed plan that guides your efforts and keeps you on track. SMART goals provide clarity, direction, and motivation, which are essential for overcoming procrastination and self-doubt.

Let's consider an example of how setting clear goals can transform your approach. Imagine you have a goal to improve your health. Instead of a vague goal like "I want to be healthier," you set a specific, measurable, achievable, relevant, and time-bound goal: "I will lose 10 pounds in three months by exercising for 30 minutes five times a week and following a balanced diet." This clear goal gives you a concrete target and a plan of action. You can track your progress, adjust your strategies as needed, and celebrate your achievements along the way.

Clear goals also provide a sense of purpose and direction. They give meaning to your efforts and help you stay focused on what truly matters. When you have a clear goal, you can filter out distractions and prioritize your actions. This sense of purpose enhances your motivation and drive, making it easier to stay committed to your objectives.

Understanding the importance of clear goals is the first step towards building confidence and overcoming procrastination. Clear goals provide direction, purpose, and a sense of accomplishment. They help you stay focused, motivated, and resilient in the face of challenges. By setting specific, measurable, achievable, relevant, and time-bound goals, you can create a roadmap for success and take meaningful steps towards achieving your dreams. The journey of a thousand miles begins with a single step.

Set your goals, take that first step, and watch your dreams come to life.

2: Defining Your Objectives

Defining your objectives is one of the most crucial steps in achieving your goals and overcoming procrastination and self-doubt. It's the process of turning vague ideas and dreams into clear, actionable targets. By clearly defining what you want to achieve, you create a roadmap that guides your actions and decisions, making it easier to stay focused and motivated.

Think about your objectives as the foundation of your journey. Without a solid foundation, it's easy for your plans to fall apart. Vague objectives like "I want to be successful" or "I want to be happier" are difficult to pursue because they lack clarity. Instead, you need to be specific about what success or happiness looks like for you. What exactly do you want to achieve? The more specific you can be, the better.

For example, if your goal is to be healthier, ask yourself what that means to you. Is it about losing weight, eating better, exercising more, or perhaps all of these? By breaking down the concept of "being healthier" into specific objectives, you create a clear target to aim for. Instead of the vague goal of "being healthier," you might define your objectives as "losing 10 pounds in three months," "eating five servings of vegetables every day," and "exercising for 30 minutes five times a week."

Being specific about your objectives also involves considering the details. For instance, if your goal is to start a new career, think about what that career looks like. What industry are you interested in? What role do you see yourself in? What steps do you need to take to make this transition? By answering these questions, you can turn a broad goal into a series of specific, actionable steps.

Once you have a clear idea of what you want to achieve, it's important to make your objectives measurable. This means defining how you will track your progress and know when you've achieved your goal. Measurable objectives provide a way to quantify your efforts and see tangible results, which is crucial for maintaining motivation.

For example, if your goal is to improve your fitness, a measurable objective might be "to run a 5K in under 30 minutes within six months." This objective is specific and gives you a clear way to measure your progress. You can track your running times and see how you improve over time. This not only helps you stay motivated but also provides a sense of accomplishment as you see your efforts paying off.

It's also important to ensure your objectives are achievable. While it's great to aim high, setting goals that are too ambitious can lead to frustration and discouragement. Achievable objectives take into account your current abilities and resources, allowing for incremental progress that builds confidence.

For instance, if you're new to exercise, setting a goal to run a marathon in three months might be unrealistic. Instead, an achievable objective could be to run a 5K in three months, with a longer-term goal of running a marathon in a year. This way, you set yourself up for success by creating objectives that are challenging yet attainable.

Relevance is another key component of defining your objectives. Your goals should align with your values and long-term aspirations, providing a sense of purpose and meaning. When setting objectives, consider why they matter to you. How do they fit into your overall vision for your life? Goals that are relevant and personally meaningful are more likely to keep you engaged and committed.

For example, if you value creativity and self-expression, an objective related to starting a creative project, like writing a book or launching an art exhibit, will be more motivating than one that doesn't resonate with your core values. Ensuring your objectives are relevant helps to maintain your intrinsic motivation and drive.

Finally, time-bound objectives create a sense of urgency and help you prioritize your actions. Without a deadline, goals can easily be postponed indefinitely. Time-bound objectives provide a clear timeline for achieving your goals, encouraging consistent effort and progress.

For example, if your goal is to complete a professional certification, setting a time-bound objective like "to pass the certification exam within six months" gives you a specific timeframe to work within. This helps you to stay focused and accountable, ensuring that you make steady progress towards your goal.

Defining your objectives also involves breaking them down into smaller, manageable tasks. Large goals can feel overwhelming, but when you break them into smaller steps, they become much more attainable. Each task becomes a stepping stone towards your larger objective, allowing you to make steady progress without feeling overwhelmed.

For example, if your objective is to write a book, break it down into smaller tasks like outlining the chapters, writing a certain number of words each day, and revising one chapter at a time. This approach makes the process less daunting and allows you to celebrate small victories along the way, keeping you motivated and engaged.

By clearly defining your objectives, you create a solid foundation for achieving your goals. You know exactly what you're working towards, how you will measure your progress, and the steps you need to take. This clarity reduces the uncertainty and overwhelm that often lead to procrastination and self-doubt.

Defining your objectives is a critical step in achieving your goals and overcoming procrastination and self-doubt. By setting specific, measurable, achievable, relevant, and time-bound objectives, you create a clear roadmap that guides your actions and decisions. This clarity provides direction, motivation, and a sense of accomplishment as you make progress towards your goals. The journey to achieving your dreams starts with clearly defined objectives.

Take the time to define your objectives, break them down into manageable tasks, and watch as your dreams become reality.

3: Breaking Down Goals into Manageable Tasks

Once you have clear objectives, the next step is to break them down into smaller, manageable tasks. This is where the magic happens. Large goals can feel overwhelming and unattainable, but when you break them down into smaller tasks, they become much more manageable. It's like turning a seemingly insurmountable mountain into a series of smaller, climbable hills.

Think of each task as a stepping stone on your path to success. For example, if one of your objectives is to develop a business plan, break it down into smaller tasks like researching business plans, outlining your plan, and writing each section step-by-step. This approach not only makes the process less daunting but also allows you to celebrate small victories along the way, keeping you motivated and engaged.

Let's delve deeper into this process. Imagine you have a large, ambitious goal that you are passionate about. The enormity of this goal can be paralyzing, leading to procrastination and self-doubt. By breaking it down into smaller, actionable tasks, you create a clear path forward, making it easier to see progress and maintain momentum. This methodical approach transforms an overwhelming goal into a series of achievable steps, each bringing you closer to your ultimate objective.

Identify

The first step is to identify and list all the components of your goal. This is where you brainstorm and write down everything you need to do to achieve your objective. Take the business plan example again. Start by listing all the elements that a comprehensive business plan should include executive summary, market analysis, company description, organizational structure, product line or services, marketing and sales strategy, funding request, and financial projections. By breaking the goal down into these components, you create a structured plan that's easier to manage.

Make Smaller

Next, take each component and break it down further into smaller tasks. For instance, under market analysis, you might list tasks such as researching industry trends, identifying your target market, analysing competitors, and gathering customer insights. Each of these tasks can be tackled individually, making the larger goal of completing a market analysis more achievable.

This method works for any goal, whether it's writing a book, getting fit, learning a new skill, or starting a business. Suppose your goal is to run a marathon. The idea of running 26.2 miles can be daunting, especially if you're new to running. However, by breaking it down into smaller tasks, the goal becomes much more achievable. Start with a manageable task, like running for 10 minutes three times a week. Gradually increase your running time and frequency, setting small, incremental goals along the way. Celebrate each milestone, such as running your first mile without stopping or completing a 5K race. These small achievements keep you motivated and reinforce your progress.

Another example might be learning a new language. If your goal is to become fluent in Spanish, breaking it down into smaller tasks makes it more manageable. Begin with basic vocabulary and phrases, then move on to more complex grammar and sentence structures. Set specific tasks, such as learning 10 new words a day or practicing conversational skills with a language partner. By focusing on these smaller tasks, you'll gradually build your language skills and move closer to fluency.

It's also essential to prioritize your tasks. Not all tasks are equally important, and some will have a greater impact on your progress than others. Identify the most critical tasks that will move you closer to your goal and tackle those first. This is often referred to as the 80/20 rule or Pareto Principle, which suggests that 80% of your results come from 20% of your efforts. Focus on the tasks that will yield the highest returns and prioritize them in your action plan.

To stay organized, consider using tools like to-do lists, planners, or project management apps. These tools can help you keep track of your tasks, set deadlines, and monitor your progress. Breaking down your goals into smaller tasks and organizing them in a systematized way makes it easier to stay on track and avoid feeling overwhelmed.

Breaking down your goals into manageable tasks also allows you to identify and address potential challenges early on. For instance, while writing your business plan, you might realize you need more detailed financial projections. Recognizing this early gives you the opportunity to seek help from an accountant or financial advisor, ensuring your business plan is comprehensive and accurate.

The key to breaking down goals into manageable tasks is to maintain flexibility and adaptability. Life is unpredictable, and sometimes unexpected challenges or opportunities arise. Being able to adjust your tasks and timelines as needed is crucial for maintaining progress. For example, if you encounter an obstacle that slows down your progress, reassess your plan and adjust your tasks and deadlines accordingly. This flexibility ensures that you stay on track without becoming discouraged by setbacks.

Celebrate your progress along the way. Recognizing and celebrating small victories is essential for maintaining motivation. Each time you complete a task, take a moment to acknowledge your achievement. This positive reinforcement helps build momentum and encourages you to keep moving forward. Celebrating your progress doesn't have to be elaborate; it can be as simple as taking a break, treating yourself to something you enjoy, or sharing your success with a friend or mentor.

Another crucial aspect of breaking down goals into manageable tasks is the psychological boost it provides. Large goals can feel overwhelming and lead to feelings of anxiety and self-doubt. By focusing on smaller, achievable tasks, you create a sense of accomplishment and build confidence in your abilities. Each completed task serves as a reminder of your capability and progress, reinforcing your belief that you can achieve your larger goal.

Visualizing your progress can also be a powerful motivator. Consider creating a visual representation of your tasks and progress, such as a progress chart or vision board. This visual reminder serves as a constant source of motivation and inspiration, helping you stay focused on your goal. Seeing your progress visually can be incredibly satisfying and encourage you to keep pushing forward.

Breaking down your goals into manageable tasks also enhances your time management skills. By identifying specific tasks and setting deadlines, you create a structured plan that helps you allocate your time more effectively. This approach prevents procrastination and ensures that you make steady progress towards your goal. Effective time management is essential for balancing your goals with other responsibilities and commitments, ensuring that you stay on track without feeling overwhelmed.

Moreover, breaking down your goals into smaller tasks allows you to measure your progress more accurately. It's easier to track and evaluate your progress when you have clear, specific tasks to complete. This measurement helps you stay accountable and provides valuable insights into what's working and what needs adjustment. Regularly reviewing your progress and making necessary adjustments ensures that you stay aligned with your objectives and continue moving forward.

Breaking down your goals into manageable tasks fosters a growth mindset. This mindset encourages you to view challenges as opportunities for learning and growth rather than obstacles. By focusing on smaller tasks and celebrating your progress, you develop resilience and perseverance. This growth mindset empowers you to tackle even the most ambitious goals with confidence and determination.

Also breaking down goals into manageable tasks is a powerful strategy for turning your ambitions into reality. By dissecting your larger goals into smaller, actionable steps, you make the journey more manageable and less overwhelming. This approach helps you stay motivated, build confidence, and maintain progress towards your objectives.

Each small step you take brings you closer to your larger goal, and every achievement, no matter how small, is a victory worth celebrating. Embrace this method and watch as your goals transform from daunting challenges into attainable successes.

4: Creating a Roadmap for Success

Now that you have your objectives and tasks outlined, it's time to create a roadmap. A roadmap is essentially a timeline that outlines when and how you will complete each task. This helps to keep you organized and ensures that you're making steady progress towards your goals. Creating a roadmap for success is about turning your vision into a structured plan that guides you step by step toward your ultimate objective.

Start by setting deadlines for each task. Be realistic about the time you have available and the effort each task requires. It's better to set achievable deadlines than to rush and feel overwhelmed. Remember, the goal is to make steady progress, not to complete everything at once. Deadlines provide a sense of urgency and help you stay on track, but they should be realistic and considerate of your overall schedule and other commitments.

Use tools that work best for you, whether it's a planner, a digital calendar, or project management software. These tools can help you visualize your timeline and keep all your tasks organized in one place. For some, a simple paper planner might be the best fit, while others might prefer a digital solution like Google Calendar, Trello, or Asana. Choose what works best for you and stick with it. The consistency of using a single tool will help you maintain clarity and focus.

Regularly review your roadmap to track your progress and make adjustments as needed. Life can be unpredictable, and it's okay to revise your plan to accommodate changes. The key is to stay flexible and committed to your overall objectives. Regular reviews allow you to reflect on what's working, what isn't, and where you need to make changes. This adaptive approach ensures that your roadmap remains a relevant and effective guide.

When setting deadlines, consider the effort each task requires. Some tasks will naturally take more time and energy than others. Break larger tasks into smaller, more manageable sub-tasks, and allocate time for each. This approach prevents you from feeling overwhelmed and helps you maintain a steady pace. For example, if your goal is to write a book, break it down into chapters and then further into daily word count goals. Allocate specific times each day or week dedicated solely to writing.

Recognise and Celebrate the Small Victories

Celebrate your progress along the way. Recognizing and celebrating small victories is essential for maintaining motivation. Each time you complete a task, take a moment to acknowledge your achievement. This positive reinforcement helps build momentum and encourages you to keep moving forward. Celebrating your progress doesn't have to be elaborate; it can be as simple as taking a break, treating yourself to something you enjoy, or sharing your success with a friend or mentor.

A roadmap for success also includes anticipating potential obstacles and planning how to overcome them. Life is full of unexpected events that can derail your progress if you're not prepared. Think about what might hinder your progress and develop strategies to address these challenges. This proactive approach helps you stay resilient and adaptable, ensuring that you remain on track even when faced with difficulties.

Incorporate buffer times in your roadmap. These are extra periods built into your timeline to account for unforeseen delays or additional time needed to complete tasks. Buffer times provide a cushion that prevents you from falling behind schedule due to unexpected events or challenges. They also reduce stress by giving you a sense of flexibility and control over your timeline.

Stay committed to your overall objectives by keeping your vision in mind. Visual reminders of your goals, such as vision boards or written affirmations, can keep you focused and motivated. Place these reminders in visible locations where you'll see them daily. They serve as constant motivation and reinforce your commitment to your roadmap.

Communication is also an important aspect of maintaining your roadmap. Share your goals and progress with a trusted friend, mentor, or accountability partner. Discussing your plans and receiving feedback can provide valuable insights and encouragement. It also adds a layer of accountability, as you're more likely to stay committed to your roadmap when someone else is aware of your goals and progress.

Always Put Yourself First

Another key aspect of creating a roadmap is prioritizing self-care. Achieving your goals should not come at the expense of your health and well-being. Ensure that your roadmap includes time for rest, relaxation, and activities that rejuvenate you. This balance is crucial for maintaining long-term productivity and avoiding burnout.

Use milestones to mark significant points in your journey. Milestones are larger goals within your roadmap that signify major progress. Reaching a milestone is a time for celebration and reflection. It's a chance to look back at how far you've come and to refocus on the next phase of your journey. Milestones provide a sense of accomplishment and help maintain motivation.

Reviewing your roadmap also involves being honest with yourself about what's working and what isn't. If you find that certain tasks consistently take longer than expected, or if you're struggling to stay motivated, take a step back and reassess your approach. Maybe you need to break tasks down even further, adjust your deadlines, or seek additional support. The goal is to create a roadmap that works for you, not against you.

Remember that a roadmap is a living document. It's meant to evolve and adapt as you make progress and as circumstances change. Regularly update your roadmap to reflect your current situation and goals. This flexibility ensures that your plan remains relevant and effective, guiding you steadily towards success.

Creating a roadmap for success involves setting realistic deadlines, using effective tools, regularly reviewing and adjusting your plan, anticipating obstacles, incorporating buffer times, staying committed to your vision, prioritizing self-care, using milestones, and being flexible. By following these principles, you can turn your objectives into actionable steps and maintain steady progress towards your goals.

Your roadmap is your guide, helping you navigate the journey and ensuring that you stay on track and motivated.

Success is not a destination but a journey, and your roadmap is a crucial tool for making that journey a successful one.

5: Overcoming Obstacles and Staying Motivated

As you work towards your goals, it's natural to encounter obstacles and moments of doubt. This is where self-awareness and resilience come into play. When you face challenges, remind yourself of why you set these goals in the first place. Reflect on your motivations and the benefits of achieving your objectives. Keeping this in mind will help you stay focused and committed, even when the going gets tough.

Stay connected to your progress by celebrating small achievements. Each task you complete brings you one step closer to your goal. Use these moments to boost your confidence and reinforce your commitment. Share your progress with a supportive friend or mentor who can provide encouragement and accountability. Celebrating small wins is crucial for maintaining motivation. These celebrations don't have to be elaborate; even a simple acknowledgment of your achievements can provide a significant boost.

One effective way to overcome obstacles is to break them down into smaller, manageable parts, just as you do with your goals. By tackling one aspect of the challenge at a time, you make it more manageable and less intimidating. This approach also helps you maintain a sense of control and progress, which can be incredibly motivating.

Another important strategy is to maintain a positive mindset. Challenges and setbacks are a natural part of any journey, but how you respond to them makes all the difference. Instead of viewing obstacles as insurmountable barriers, see them as opportunities for growth and learning. This shift in perspective can help you stay motivated and resilient. Remind yourself that every challenge you overcome strengthens your skills and brings you closer to your goal.

Resilience is key when facing obstacles. It's about bouncing back from setbacks and continuing to move forward, even when things don't go as planned. Developing resilience involves building a strong foundation of self-belief and perseverance. One way to do this is by reflecting on past challenges you've overcome and reminding yourself of your ability to navigate difficult situations. Drawing on these experiences can help you build confidence and stay motivated when faced with new obstacles.

Mindfulness and self-awareness are also valuable tools in maintaining motivation. By staying present and aware of your thoughts and emotions, you can better manage stress and stay focused on your goals. Mindfulness practices, such as meditation and deep breathing exercises, can help you stay grounded and reduce anxiety. These practices also enhance your ability to stay positive and resilient in the face of challenges.

When obstacles arise, it's important to be flexible and adaptable. Sometimes, your initial plan may need to be adjusted to accommodate new circumstances. Being open to change and willing to revise your approach can help you navigate obstacles more effectively. This flexibility ensures that you stay on track, even when unexpected challenges occur.

Share Your Life with Those That Share Your Goals

Seeking support from others is another crucial aspect of overcoming obstacles and staying motivated. Surround yourself with positive, encouraging people who believe in you and your goals. Share your challenges and progress with them, and don't be afraid to ask for help when needed. Having a strong support network can provide valuable insights, encouragement, and accountability. It's also beneficial to learn from others who have faced similar challenges and successfully overcome them.

Accountability partners can be particularly helpful in maintaining motivation. Having someone to share your goals with and report your progress can create a sense of responsibility and commitment. Your accountability partner can offer encouragement, provide feedback, and help you stay focused on your objectives. This mutual support system can be incredibly motivating and help you stay on track.

It's also important to take care of your physical and mental well-being. Proper self-care is essential for maintaining the energy and focus needed to overcome obstacles and stay motivated. Ensure that you're getting enough sleep, eating a balanced diet, and engaging in regular physical activity. Taking breaks and giving yourself time to rest and recharge can prevent burnout and keep you motivated over the long term.

Journaling can be a powerful tool for staying motivated and overcoming obstacles. By regularly writing down your thoughts, feelings, and progress, you create a record of your journey that you can reflect on. Journaling allows you to track your progress, celebrate your successes, and analyse any challenges you encounter. It also provides an opportunity for self-reflection, helping you gain insights into your motivations and how to address any obstacles that arise.

Visualization is another effective technique for maintaining motivation. By visualizing your success and imagining the positive outcomes of achieving your goals, you reinforce your commitment and boost your confidence. Spend a few minutes each day visualizing yourself overcoming obstacles and reaching your objectives. This practice can enhance your motivation and help you stay focused on your goals.

Sometimes, obstacles may seem overwhelming, and it's easy to lose sight of your progress. In these moments, it's helpful to break down your journey into smaller milestones. Focus on the next small step you need to take rather than the entire path ahead. This approach makes the journey feel more manageable and keeps you moving forward. Each small step you take is a victory and brings you closer to your goal.

Maintaining a sense of purpose can also help you stay motivated. Reflect on why your goals are important to you and how achieving them will impact your life and the lives of others. Connecting your actions to a larger purpose can provide a powerful source of motivation and keep you focused on overcoming any obstacles that arise.

*Obstacles Are Only Encountered If
You Are Moving Forward*

Remember that setbacks are a natural part of any journey. It's important not to be too hard on yourself when things don't go as planned. Treat yourself with kindness and compassion and use setbacks as learning opportunities. Analyse what went wrong, identify any lessons learned, and apply these insights to your future efforts. This proactive approach helps you grow stronger and more resilient with each challenge you face.

Another helpful strategy is to set short-term, achievable goals alongside your long-term objectives. These short-term goals provide immediate targets to aim for and offer frequent opportunities for success and celebration. Achieving these smaller goals can boost your motivation and provide a sense of accomplishment that propels you forward.

Staying motivated also involves maintaining a healthy work-life balance. Ensure that you're making time for activities you enjoy and that bring you joy and fulfilment. Engaging in hobbies, spending time with loved ones, and taking time for relaxation and self-care are all important for maintaining your overall well-being and motivation.

Overcoming obstacles and staying motivated requires a combination of self-awareness, resilience, and strategic planning. By breaking down challenges into manageable parts, maintaining a positive mindset, seeking support, and taking care of your well-being, you can navigate obstacles effectively and stay committed to your goals. Celebrate your progress, stay connected to your purpose, and remain flexible and adaptable in your approach.

Each step you take, no matter how small, is a step towards success. With determination and perseverance, you can overcome any obstacle and achieve your objectives. Stay motivated, stay focused, and keep moving forward on your journey to success.

6: Building Confidence Through Action

Taking consistent action towards your goals is the best way to build confidence. Each step you take, no matter how small, is a testament to your commitment and capability. As you make progress, you'll find that your self-doubt diminishes, and your confidence grows. This process of building confidence through action is both transformative and empowering, allowing you to realize your potential and achieve your aspirations.

The journey towards achieving your goals is just as important as the destination. Embrace the process, learn from setbacks, and celebrate your growth. By setting clear and achievable goals, breaking them down into manageable tasks, and creating a roadmap for success, you're building a solid foundation for personal and professional growth.

Imagine that you have a goal to learn a new skill, such as public speaking. The idea of speaking in front of a large audience may initially seem daunting and filled with uncertainty. However, by breaking this goal into smaller, actionable steps, you can start building your confidence gradually. Begin with something manageable, like practicing your speech in front of a mirror or a small group of friends. Each time you practice, you gain a bit more confidence and become more comfortable with the process.

One Small Step

The first step is often the hardest, but it's also the most important. Taking that initial step, regardless of how small it might seem, is a significant milestone. It represents your commitment to your goal and sets the stage for continued progress. Each subsequent step becomes a little easier, and before you know it, you're making strides towards your objective.

Consistency is key when it comes to building confidence. Regular, repeated actions help to reinforce your abilities and solidify your self-belief. Consider the example of learning to play a musical instrument. Initially, you might struggle with basic chords or notes, but with consistent practice, you gradually improve. Each successful practice session builds on the previous one, leading to increased skill and confidence.

As you continue to act, it's important to acknowledge and celebrate your achievements, no matter how small they may seem. Celebrating your progress reinforces positive behaviour and boosts your motivation. It reminds you of how far you've come and encourages you to keep moving forward. This positive reinforcement is crucial for maintaining momentum and building lasting confidence.

Setbacks are an inevitable part of any journey, but they don't have to derail your progress. Instead, view setbacks as opportunities for learning and growth. Each challenge you encounter provides valuable insights and lessons that can help you improve. Embracing setbacks with a positive mindset allows you to build resilience and adaptability, both of which are essential for long-term success.

One powerful way to build confidence through action is to set clear and achievable goals. Specific, measurable goals provide a sense of direction and purpose. They help you focus your efforts and track your progress. When setting goals, ensure they are realistic and attainable. Overly ambitious goals can lead to frustration and self-doubt, while achievable goals provide a steady stream of successes that boost your confidence.

Breaking down your goals into manageable tasks makes them more attainable and less overwhelming. For instance, if your goal is to write a book, break it down into smaller tasks such as outlining the chapters, writing a certain number of words each day, and editing each section. This approach allows you to make consistent progress and keeps you engaged with the process.

Creating a roadmap for success further enhances your confidence. A roadmap outlines the steps you need to take to achieve your goals and provides a clear timeline for completion. It helps you stay organized and focused, ensuring that you're consistently moving forward. Regularly reviewing and adjusting your roadmap allows you to stay on track and make necessary changes based on your progress.

Taking action also involves stepping out of your comfort zone. Growth and confidence come from challenging yourself and pushing beyond your limits. While this can be uncomfortable at times, it's essential for personal development. Each time you take a risk or try something new, you expand your capabilities and build confidence in your ability to handle uncertainty.

Consider the example of starting a new job. The first few days or weeks may be filled with uncertainty and self-doubt as you navigate new responsibilities and a different work environment. However, as you become more familiar with your role and gain experience, your confidence grows. You become more comfortable in your position and more assured in your abilities.

Mindfulness and self-awareness play a crucial role in building confidence through action. By staying present and attentive to your thoughts and emotions, you can better manage stress and stay focused on your goals. Mindfulness practices, such as meditation and deep breathing exercises, can help you stay grounded and maintain a positive mindset. These practices enhance your ability to stay resilient and confident, even in the face of challenges.

All Feedback Is Useful.
Especially If It's Not Meant to Be.

Another important aspect of building confidence through action is seeking feedback and support from others. Surround yourself with positive, encouraging people who believe in you and your goals. Share your progress with them and seek their feedback. Constructive feedback can provide valuable insights and help you improve, while encouragement and support boost your motivation and confidence.

Accountability partners can be particularly beneficial in maintaining your commitment to taking action. An accountability partner is someone who shares your goals and holds you accountable for your progress. This mutual support system creates a sense of responsibility and commitment, helping you stay on track and motivated.

It's also essential to take care of your physical and mental well-being. Proper self-care is crucial for maintaining the energy and focus needed to take consistent action towards your goals. Ensure that you're getting enough sleep, eating a balanced diet, and engaging in regular physical activity. Taking breaks and giving yourself time to rest and recharge prevents burnout and keeps you motivated over the long term.

Visualization is another powerful tool for building confidence through action. By visualizing your success and imagining the positive outcomes of achieving your goals, you reinforce your commitment and boost your confidence. Spend a few minutes each day visualizing yourself taking action and reaching your objectives. This practice enhances your motivation and helps you stay focused on your goals.

Maintaining a sense of purpose can also help you stay motivated and confident. Reflect on why your goals are important to you and how achieving them will impact your life and the lives of others. Connecting your actions to a larger purpose provides a powerful source of motivation and keeps you focused on taking consistent action.

Remember that building confidence through action is a continuous journey. It's not about achieving perfection but about making steady progress and growing along the way. Each step you take, no matter how small, is a step towards success. Embrace the process, celebrate your achievements, and learn from setbacks. By taking consistent action, you're building a solid foundation for personal and professional growth.

Building confidence through action involves taking consistent steps towards your goals, embracing the journey, and celebrating your progress. By setting clear and achievable goals, breaking them down into manageable tasks, and creating a roadmap for success, you create a structured path to follow. Staying mindful, seeking feedback, and taking care of your well-being further enhance your ability to take action and build confidence.

Each step you take is a testament to your commitment and capability, bringing you closer to your goals and helping you realize your full potential.

7: Take Out

Setting clear, specific, and achievable goals is a powerful strategy for overcoming procrastination and self-doubt. By defining your objectives, breaking them down into manageable tasks, and creating a roadmap for success, you can make consistent progress and build confidence with each step. Remember, the journey is a process, and each small victory is a testament to your dedication and resilience. Let's continue this journey together, one step at a time.

When you set clear and specific goals, you give yourself a tangible target to aim for. Vague goals can be overwhelming and difficult to achieve, leading to procrastination and self-doubt. By defining your objectives in precise terms, you create a roadmap that guides your actions and helps you stay focused. For instance, instead of setting a goal to "get fit," specify that you want to "run a 5K in three months." This specificity gives you a clear endpoint and a sense of direction.

Breaking down these goals into manageable tasks makes the process less daunting and more achievable. Large goals can feel overwhelming, leading to procrastination as you struggle to figure out where to start. By dividing your objectives into smaller, actionable steps, you create a series of tasks that are easier to tackle. This approach allows you to focus on one step at a time, reducing the feeling of being overwhelmed and increasing your chances of success.

Creating a roadmap for success further enhances your ability to achieve your goals. A roadmap outlines the steps you need to take and provides a timeline for completion. This structured approach helps you stay organized and ensures that you are making consistent progress. Regularly reviewing and adjusting your roadmap allows you to stay on track and make necessary changes as you move forward. Flexibility is key, as life is unpredictable, and being able to adapt your plan to accommodate changes is crucial for maintaining momentum.

Each small victory along the way is a testament to your dedication and resilience. Celebrating these achievements, no matter how minor they may seem, reinforces positive behaviour and boosts your confidence. These celebrations provide a sense of accomplishment and motivate you to keep moving forward. Remember, progress is progress, no matter the size, and acknowledging your efforts helps maintain your motivation and commitment.

Enjoy The Journey

The journey towards achieving your goals is just as important as the destination. Embrace the process, learn from setbacks, and celebrate your growth. Setbacks and challenges are a natural part of any journey, and they provide valuable learning opportunities. Instead of viewing them as failures, see them as stepping stones that contribute to your overall development. Each challenge you overcome strengthens your resilience and builds your confidence.

It's important to stay connected to your progress and remain aware of your motivations. Reflecting on why you set your goals in the first place and the benefits of achieving them helps you stay focused and committed. This reflection keeps you grounded and reminds you of the bigger picture, especially during challenging times. Keeping your motivations in mind fuels your drive and determination, helping you push through obstacles.

Share your progress with a supportive friend or mentor who can provide encouragement and accountability. Having someone to share your journey with adds a layer of support and motivation. They can offer valuable insights, celebrate your successes with you, and help you stay accountable to your goals. This shared experience creates a sense of camaraderie and strengthens your commitment to your objectives.

Taking consistent action towards your goals is the best way to build confidence. Each step you take, no matter how small, demonstrates your capability and reinforces your self-belief. As you make progress, your self-doubt diminishes, and your confidence grows. This positive feedback loop encourages you to continue taking action and propels you forward on your journey.

Building confidence and achieving your goals is a continuous process. It's not about reaching the finish line as quickly as possible but about making steady progress and growing along the way. Each small step you take brings you closer to your larger goal and helps you develop the skills and resilience needed for long-term success.

Continue this journey one step at a time. Embrace the process, celebrate your victories, and stay committed to your goals. With each action you take, you are building a stronger, more confident version of yourself.

Keep moving forward and remember that you have the power to achieve your dreams.

Chapter 3: Developing an Action Plan

"Learn how to create an effective action plan together. This chapter provides step-by-step instructions on prioritizing tasks, setting deadlines, and using productivity tools.

The focus is on taking immediate, actionable steps to start making progress towards your goals."

Synopsis

In this chapter, you'll learn how to create an effective action plan with step-by-step instructions on prioritizing tasks, setting deadlines, and using productivity tools. The focus is on taking immediate, actionable steps to start making progress towards your goals.

Section 1: Identifying Your Goals

In this section, we'll help you clearly define your goals. You'll learn techniques for breaking down broad objectives into specific, achievable targets, setting a strong foundation for your action plan.

Section 2: Prioritizing Tasks

Discover methods for prioritizing tasks based on importance and urgency. We'll introduce tools like the Eisenhower Matrix to help you categorize tasks and focus your time and energy on what truly matters.

Section 3: Setting Deadlines

Learn the importance of setting realistic and motivating deadlines. We'll share strategies for creating a timeline that balances ambition with practicality, ensuring you make steady progress without burning out.

Section 4: Using Productivity Tools

Explore various productivity tools and apps to streamline your task management. I'll provide tips on selecting the right tools based on your preferences and goals, enhancing your efficiency and organization.

Section 5: Creating a Step-by-Step Plan

I'll guide you through developing a detailed action plan. This section includes templates and examples to help you outline tasks, assign deadlines, and track your progress effectively.

Section 6: Implementing Your Plan

Focus on taking the first steps to implement your action plan. I'll offer advice on overcoming initial resistance, staying motivated, and maintaining momentum as you begin making tangible progress towards your goals.

Section 7: Monitoring and Adjusting Your Plan

Learn how to regularly review and adjust your action plan to stay on track. This section includes techniques for monitoring progress, identifying areas for improvement, and adapting your plan to changing circumstances and new insights.

1: Identifying Your Goals

To clearly define your goals, you'll require techniques for breaking down broad objectives into specific, achievable targets, setting a strong foundation for your action plan. Understanding and identifying your goals is the first step towards a fulfilling and successful journey, and it's essential to approach this process with clarity and purpose.

Setting goals might seem straightforward, but it requires introspection and careful consideration. Start by reflecting on what truly matters to you. Think about your passions, values, and long-term aspirations. What do you want to achieve, and why is it important to you? This reflection helps you connect with your inner motivations and ensures that your goals align with your personal values and desires.

Once you have a broad idea of what you want to achieve, it's time to break it down into specific, measurable targets. Broad goals like "get healthier" or "advance my career" are too vague to provide a clear path forward. Instead, focus on specific aspects of these goals. For example, if your goal is to get healthier, consider what that means to you. Is it about losing weight, eating better, or exercising regularly? Breaking down the goal into smaller, actionable steps makes it more manageable and achievable.

Let's delve deeper into the process of setting specific goals. Use the SMART criteria to ensure your goals are well-defined. SMART stands for Specific, Measurable, Achievable, Relevant, and Time-bound. This framework helps you create clear and attainable goals.

Specific

Your goal should be clear and specific, answering the questions of who, what, where, when, and why. For instance, instead of saying "I want to be fit," specify "I want to run a 5K race in six months."

Measurable

Establish criteria for tracking your progress. This could be quantifiable metrics like numbers, dates, or specific actions. For example, "I will run three times a week and increase my distance by 10% each week."

Achievable

Ensure that your goal is realistic and attainable. It should challenge you but still be possible to achieve with effort and commitment. If you're new to running, starting with a 5K race is more achievable than aiming for a marathon.

Relevant

Your goal should align with your broader life objectives and values. Ask yourself why this goal matters to you and how it fits into your overall vision. Running a 5K might be relevant because it improves your health and provides a sense of accomplishment.

Time-bound

Set a deadline for your goal to create a sense of urgency and motivation. Having a specific timeframe helps you stay focused and committed. For example, "I will complete the 5K race by the end of June."

By applying the SMART criteria, you transform vague aspirations into concrete goals that provide a clear direction and purpose.

Next, break these specific goals into even smaller, manageable tasks. This process involves identifying the individual steps you need to take to reach your goal. For instance, preparing for a 5K race might involve tasks such as researching training plans, buying running shoes, and scheduling your runs. Each task should be small enough to be completed within a short timeframe, making it easier to track progress and maintain motivation.

Creating a visual representation of your goals can also be helpful. Consider using a vision board or a goal-setting journal where you can outline your objectives, tasks, and milestones. Visual tools provide a tangible reminder of your goals and help you stay focused and inspired.

Accountability is another crucial aspect of achieving your goals. Share your objectives with a trusted friend, family member, or mentor who can provide support and encouragement.

Regular check-ins with your accountability partner can help you stay on track and address any challenges that arise. Knowing that someone else is aware of your goals and progress adds a layer of responsibility and motivation.

As you work towards your goals, regularly review and adjust them as needed. Life is dynamic, and circumstances can change, requiring you to adapt your plans. Periodically reassess your goals to ensure they remain relevant and achievable.

Don't be afraid to modify your objectives if necessary; the key is to stay flexible and committed to your overall vision.

Celebrate your progress along the way. Each step you take, no matter how small, brings you closer to your goal. Acknowledge your efforts and reward yourself for your achievements. Celebrating your progress reinforces positive behaviour and boosts your confidence, encouraging you to keep moving forward.

Identifying your goals is a crucial first step towards personal and professional growth. By clearly defining your objectives, breaking them down into specific, achievable targets, and setting a strong foundation for your action plan, you create a roadmap for success. Stay flexible, seek support, and celebrate your progress as you journey towards your goals.

2: Prioritizing Tasks

Prioritizing tasks is a crucial skill for anyone looking to build confidence and achieve their goals. By organizing your tasks based on their importance and urgency, you can focus your time and energy on what truly matters, ensuring that you make consistent progress without feeling overwhelmed. In this section, we'll explore effective methods for prioritizing tasks, including the use of the Eisenhower Matrix, a powerful tool that can help you categorize your tasks and stay on track.

One of the most common challenges people face when working towards their goals is determining which tasks to tackle first. With numerous responsibilities vying for your attention, it's easy to feel overwhelmed and unsure where to start. This is where prioritization comes in. By systematically evaluating and ranking your tasks, you can create a clear plan of action that guides your efforts and keeps you focused.

The Eisenhower Matrix, also known as the Urgent-Important Matrix, is an excellent tool for prioritizing tasks. Named after President Dwight D. Eisenhower, who famously used this method to manage his workload, the matrix helps you categorize tasks based on their urgency and importance. It divides tasks into four quadrants:

1. Important and Urgent

Tasks that require immediate attention. These are critical activities that contribute directly to your goals and have tight deadlines. Examples include urgent work projects, crises that need resolution, and last-minute preparations.

2. Important but Not Urgent

Tasks that are important for your long-term goals but don't require immediate action. These activities contribute to your growth and success but can be scheduled for later. Examples include strategic planning, skill development, and relationship-building.

3. Urgent but Not Important

Tasks that demand immediate attention but don't significantly contribute to your goals. These activities are often distractions that prevent you from focusing on what truly matters. Examples include unnecessary meetings, minor interruptions, and low-priority emails.

4. *Not Urgent and Not Important*

Tasks that are neither urgent nor important. These activities add little value and can often be eliminated or minimized. Examples include mindless social media browsing, unproductive gossip, and other time-wasting activities.

Using the Eisenhower Matrix, you can sort your tasks into these four categories, helping you identify which ones to prioritize. Focus your efforts on tasks in the first two quadrants—those that are important and urgent, and those that are important but not urgent. These tasks should take precedence because they directly impact your goals and long-term success.

Tasks in the third quadrant—urgent but not important—should be delegated or minimized whenever possible. These activities can consume valuable time and energy, diverting your attention from more meaningful tasks. For tasks in the fourth quadrant—neither urgent nor important—consider eliminating them altogether. These activities often serve as distractions that hinder your productivity.

In addition to the Eisenhower Matrix, other prioritization techniques can help you stay organized and focused. The ABCDE method, for example, involves labelling tasks based on their priority:

A

Tasks that are very important and must be done. These tasks have serious consequences if not completed.

B

Tasks that are important but not as critical as A tasks. These tasks have mild consequences if not completed.

C

Tasks that are nice to do but don't have significant consequences if not completed.

D

Tasks that can be delegated to someone else.

E

Tasks that can be eliminated.

By assigning each task a letter, you can easily identify which ones to tackle first, and which ones can be delegated or eliminated.

Another effective method is the "Eat That Frog" technique, inspired by a quote attributed to Mark Twain: "Eat a live frog first thing in the morning, and nothing worse will happen to you the rest of the day." In this context, the "frog" represents your most important and challenging task. By tackling this task first thing in the morning, you set a positive tone for the rest of the day and ensure that you're making progress on what truly matters.

Prioritizing tasks also involves regular review and adjustment. As you complete tasks and new ones arise, it's essential to reassess your priorities and make necessary adjustments. This dynamic approach ensures that you stay aligned with your goals and can adapt to changing circumstances.

To stay organized and keep track of your priorities, consider using digital tools and apps designed for task management. Applications like Todoist, Trello, and Asana allow you to create task lists, set deadlines, and categorize tasks based on their priority. These tools provide a visual representation of your workload, making it easier to manage your time and stay focused.

Prioritizing tasks is a key strategy for building confidence and achieving your goals. By using tools like the Eisenhower Matrix, the ABCDE method, and the "Eat That Frog" technique, you can effectively organize your tasks and focus on what truly matters. Regularly reviewing and adjusting your priorities ensures that you stay on track and make consistent progress.

Remember, prioritization is not just about getting things done—it's about making sure you're doing the right things at the right time. Stay focused, stay organized, and watch as your confidence and productivity soar.

3: Setting Deadlines

Setting deadlines is a critical component of achieving your goals and building confidence. Realistic and motivating deadlines provide structure to your plans, ensuring that you make steady progress without feeling overwhelmed or burning out. In this section, we'll explore the importance of setting effective deadlines and share strategies for creating a timeline that balances ambition with practicality.

Deadlines serve as a powerful motivator, turning abstract goals into concrete actions. They create a sense of urgency and help you prioritize tasks, making it easier to focus on what needs to be done. Without deadlines, it's easy to procrastinate and lose sight of your objectives. By setting clear deadlines, you create a roadmap that guides your efforts and keeps you on track.

When setting deadlines, it's essential to be realistic about the time and effort required for each task. Overly ambitious deadlines can lead to stress and burnout, while deadlines that are too lenient may result in procrastination. Finding the right balance is key. Start by estimating how long each task will take and consider any potential obstacles or challenges that might arise. Be honest with yourself about your current commitments and availability and allocate enough time to complete each task without compromising quality or well-being.

A helpful strategy is to break down larger goals into smaller, more manageable tasks, each with its own deadline. This approach makes the overall goal less daunting and provides a series of milestones to celebrate along the way. For example, if your goal is to write a book, set deadlines for completing each chapter rather than focusing solely on the final manuscript. This method allows you to track your progress and stay motivated as you accomplish each step.

Creating a timeline for your tasks can also help you stay organized and maintain momentum. Use tools like calendars, planners, or digital apps to map out your deadlines and track your progress. Visualizing your timeline provides a clear overview of what needs to be done and when, making it easier to manage your time effectively. Regularly review and adjust your timeline as needed to accommodate any changes or unexpected events.

It's important to set deadlines that are both motivating and achievable. One way to do this is by incorporating a mix of short-term and long-term deadlines. Short-term deadlines provide immediate targets to aim for and offer frequent opportunities for success, keeping you engaged and motivated. Long-term deadlines, on the other hand, help you stay focused on your overall goal and provide a sense of direction. Balancing both types of deadlines ensures that you make consistent progress while maintaining a clear vision of your ultimate objective.

Accountability can also play a significant role in meeting deadlines. Share your goals and deadlines with a trusted friend, family member, or mentor who can provide support and encouragement. Regular check-ins with your accountability partner can help you stay on track and address any challenges that arise. Knowing that someone else is aware of your deadlines adds a layer of responsibility and motivation.

While setting deadlines is crucial, it's equally important to remain flexible and adaptable. Life is unpredictable, and circumstances can change, requiring you to adjust your plans. Be prepared to reassess your deadlines and make necessary modifications to stay aligned with your goals. This flexibility ensures that you don't become discouraged by setbacks and can continue making progress despite any obstacles.

In addition to flexibility, it's essential to practice self-compassion and patience. Achieving your goals is a journey, and it's natural to encounter setbacks along the way. Instead of being overly critical of yourself when things don't go as planned, use these moments as opportunities to learn and grow. Adjust your deadlines if needed and focus on the progress you've made rather than dwelling on any perceived shortcomings.

Celebrating your achievements is another vital aspect of setting and meeting deadlines. Acknowledge your hard work and dedication each time you reach a milestone or complete a task. These celebrations don't have to be elaborate; even a simple gesture of recognition can provide a significant boost to your motivation and confidence. Celebrating your progress reinforces positive behaviour and encourages you to continue striving towards your goals.

Setting realistic and motivating deadlines is a powerful strategy for achieving your goals and building confidence. By creating a timeline that balances ambition with practicality, you ensure steady progress without burning out. Use tools to visualize your timeline, seek support from accountability partners, and remain flexible and self-compassionate. Each deadline you meet is a step closer to your ultimate objective, and every achievement along the way is a testament to your commitment and perseverance.

Stay focused, stay motivated, and continue moving forward with confidence.

4: Using Productivity Tools

In today's fast-paced world, managing your tasks efficiently and staying organized can significantly impact your ability to achieve your goals and build confidence. Productivity tools and apps are valuable resources that can help streamline your task management, making it easier to stay on top of your responsibilities and maintain progress towards your objectives. In this section, we'll explore various productivity tools and apps, and I'll provide tips on selecting the right ones based on your preferences and goals, enhancing your efficiency and organization.

Productivity tools come in many forms, from simple to-do lists and calendars to more sophisticated project management software. The key is to find tools that align with your personal workflow and enhance your ability to manage tasks effectively. Here are some popular productivity tools and how they can help you stay organized and efficient:

1. To-Do List Apps

These apps help you create and manage task lists, ensuring that you don't overlook any important tasks. Popular to-do list apps like Todoist, Microsoft To Do, and Any.do allow you to create tasks, set deadlines, and categorize tasks based on priority. These apps are particularly useful for breaking down larger goals into smaller, manageable tasks and tracking your progress.

2. Project Management Software

For more complex projects that involve multiple tasks and deadlines, project management software like Trello, Asana, and Monday.com can be invaluable. These tools provide a visual overview of your projects, allowing you to create task boards, assign tasks to team members, set deadlines, and track progress. They are ideal for both individual and team projects, helping you stay organized and on schedule.

3. Calendar Apps

Keeping track of deadlines and appointments is crucial for effective time management. Calendar apps like Google Calendar, Apple Calendar, and Outlook Calendar allow you to schedule tasks, set reminders, and synchronize your schedule across devices. Using a calendar app helps you allocate time for each task and ensures that you stay on top of your commitments.

4. Note-Taking Apps

Capturing ideas, meeting notes, and important information is essential for staying organized. Note-taking apps like Evernote, OneNote, and Notion provide a digital space to store and organize your notes. These apps often include features like search functionality, tagging, and cloud synchronization, making it easy to access your notes from anywhere.

5. Focus and Time-Tracking Apps

Maintaining focus and managing your time effectively are key to productivity. Apps like Focus@Will, Forest, and Pomodone help you stay focused by providing background music, using the Pomodoro technique, or blocking distracting websites. Time-tracking apps like Toggl and Clockify allow you to monitor how much time you spend on each task, helping you identify areas for improvement and optimize your workflow.

Selecting the right productivity tools depends on your personal preferences and goals. Here are some tips to help you choose the best tools for your needs:

Identify Your Requirements

Start by assessing your specific needs and workflow. Are you managing complex projects with multiple tasks and deadlines? Do you need a simple way to keep track of daily tasks? Understanding your requirements will help you narrow down the options and choose tools that address your unique challenges.

Test Different Tools

Don't be afraid to experiment with different tools to find what works best for you. Many productivity apps offer free trials or basic versions, allowing you to test their features and functionality before committing to a paid plan. Use this opportunity to explore various options and determine which tools enhance your productivity and organization.

Consider Integration

Choose tools that integrate seamlessly with each other and with other software you use. For example, if you use Google Calendar for scheduling, look for to-do list or project management apps that can sync with it. Integration streamlines your workflow and ensures that all your tools work together harmoniously.

Evaluate Ease of Use

The best productivity tools are intuitive and easy to use. Avoid overly complicated apps that require a steep learning curve, as they can hinder rather than enhance your productivity. Opt for tools with user-friendly interfaces and clear instructions.

Prioritize Mobility

If you're frequently on the go, choose tools that offer mobile apps or cloud-based functionality. This allows you to access your tasks, schedule, and notes from any device, ensuring that you stay organized and productive no matter where you are.

Review and Adjust

Regularly review your use of productivity tools to ensure they continue to meet your needs. As your goals and workflow evolve, you may need to adjust your toolset. Stay flexible and open to trying new tools that can further enhance your efficiency and organization.

Productivity tools and apps can significantly enhance your ability to manage tasks, stay organized, and achieve your goals. By selecting the right tools based on your preferences and goals, you can streamline your task management and boost your efficiency. Identify your requirements, test different tools, consider integration, evaluate ease of use, prioritize mobility, and regularly review and adjust your toolset.

With the right productivity tools, you'll be well-equipped to stay on track and make steady progress towards your objectives.

5: Creating a Step-by-Step Plan

Creating a step-by-step plan is a crucial aspect of achieving your goals and building confidence. A detailed action plan serves as a roadmap, guiding you through each stage of your journey and helping you stay organized and focused. In this section, I'll guide you through developing a detailed action plan, including templates and examples to help you outline tasks, assign deadlines, and track your progress effectively.

The first step in creating a step-by-step plan is to clearly define your end goal. Having a clear vision of what you want to achieve provides direction and purpose. Once you have your end goal in mind, you can start breaking it down into smaller, more manageable tasks. This process of decomposition makes your goal less overwhelming and provides a series of actionable steps that you can follow.

Begin by listing all the tasks required to achieve your goal. Think about every aspect of the project and write down each task, no matter how small. This comprehensive list will serve as the foundation of your action plan. For example, if your goal is to write a book, your task list might include brainstorming ideas, creating an outline, researching, writing each chapter, and editing.

Next, organize these tasks in a logical sequence. Consider the order in which tasks need to be completed and any dependencies between them. Some tasks may need to be done before others can start. Creating a logical flow ensures that you don't miss any critical steps and that you can make steady progress. Continuing with the book example, you would likely start with brainstorming and outlining before moving on to writing and editing.

Once you have an ordered list of tasks, it's time to assign deadlines. Setting deadlines is essential for maintaining momentum and ensuring that you stay on track. Be realistic about the time required for each task and consider any potential obstacles or challenges that might arise. It's better to set achievable deadlines than to rush and risk burnout. Use the SMART criteria (Specific, Measurable, Achievable, Relevant, and Time-bound) to set effective deadlines.

To help you organize your tasks and deadlines, consider using templates. Here's a simple template to get you started:

Action Plan Template

Goal: [Insert your goal here]

Task	Deadline	Notes
Task 1	[Deadline]	[Notes]
Task 2	[Deadline]	[Notes]
Task 3	[Deadline]	[Notes]
...	...	...

This template provides a clear overview of your tasks and deadlines, making it easier to track your progress. You can customize it to suit your needs, adding columns for priorities, status updates, or any other information that might be helpful.

Tracking your progress is another essential component of a successful action plan. Regularly reviewing your progress allows you to see how far you've come and identify any areas that need adjustment.

Use tools like checklists, calendars, or digital apps to monitor your progress and stay organized. Checking off completed tasks provides a sense of accomplishment and motivates you to keep going.

To illustrate the process, let's consider an example goal: preparing for a marathon. Here's how you might create a step-by-step plan:

Goal: Prepare for and complete a marathon in six months

Task	Deadline	Notes
Research marathon training plans	Week 1	Find a plan that suits your fitness level and schedule
Purchase running gear	Week 1	Invest in good running shoes and clothing
Start training plan	Week 2	Follow the plan's schedule for daily runs
Schedule a medical check-up	Week 2	Ensure you're in good health to start training
Track weekly progress	Weekly	Adjust plan if needed based on performance
Increase long run distance	Bi-weekly	Gradually build endurance
Participate in a half-marathon	Month 3	Gain experience in a race setting
Maintain balanced diet	Ongoing	Support training with proper nutrition
Rest and recover	Ongoing	Include rest days in the training plan
Finalize race day logistics	Month 5	Plan travel, accommodation, and race strategy
Complete marathon	Month 6	Achieve the goal!

This example demonstrates how breaking down a broad goal into specific tasks, setting deadlines, and tracking progress can help you stay organized and focused. Each task is a step towards the larger goal, making the overall process more manageable.

Another valuable tool is the Gantt chart, a visual representation of your action plan that shows tasks along a timeline. Gantt charts are especially useful for more complex projects with multiple tasks and dependencies. They provide a clear overview of your project's schedule and help you identify potential bottlenecks or delays. Many project management software options, like Trello, Asana, and Microsoft Project, offer Gantt chart features to help you visualize your plan.

As you work through your action plan, it's important to remain flexible and adaptable. Life is unpredictable, and circumstances can change, requiring you to adjust your plan. Regularly review your tasks and deadlines and be prepared to make modifications as needed. This flexibility ensures that you can stay on track even when faced with unexpected challenges.

Always celebrate your progress along the way. Acknowledge your hard work and dedication each time you reach a milestone or complete a task. Celebrating your achievements reinforces positive behaviour and boosts your confidence, encouraging you to continue striving towards your goals.

Creating a step-by-step plan is a powerful strategy for achieving your goals and building confidence. By breaking down broad objectives into specific tasks, setting deadlines, and tracking your progress, you can stay organized and focused on your journey. Use templates and tools to streamline your planning process, remain flexible and adaptable, and celebrate your progress along the way.

With a detailed action plan, you'll be well-equipped to make steady progress and achieve your goals with confidence.

6: Implementing Your Plan

Once you've created a detailed action plan, the next crucial step is to implement it. This is where you turn your carefully laid out plans into tangible actions, bringing you closer to achieving your goals. Implementing your plan can be both exciting and daunting, especially when you face initial resistance or fear of the unknown. In this section, we'll focus on taking the first steps, overcoming initial resistance, staying motivated, and maintaining momentum as you make progress toward your goals.

Taking the First Steps

The first steps in implementing your plan are often the hardest. The key is to start small and build up gradually. Begin with the easiest tasks on your list to create a sense of accomplishment and build confidence. These initial successes can provide the motivation needed to tackle more challenging tasks. Remember, every small step counts and contributes to your overall progress.

Set yourself up for success by creating a conducive environment for productivity. Organize your workspace, eliminate distractions, and gather any resources you might need. A well-prepared environment can make it easier to focus and take action.

Overcoming Initial Resistance

It's natural to encounter resistance when starting something new. This resistance can come in many forms, such as procrastination, self-doubt, or fear of failure. The first step to overcoming resistance is to acknowledge it. Recognize that feeling hesitant or anxious is normal and doesn't mean you're not capable of achieving your goals.

To combat procrastination, break down tasks into smaller, more manageable chunks. This approach makes tasks seem less overwhelming and helps you build momentum. Use techniques like the Pomodoro Technique, where you work for 25 minutes and then take a 5-minute break, to maintain focus and productivity.

Self-doubt can be a significant barrier to action. Counteract negative self-talk with positive affirmations and remind yourself of your past successes. Surround yourself with supportive people who believe in your abilities and can offer encouragement when you need it.

Fear of failure is another common form of resistance. Reframe failure as a learning opportunity rather than a setback. Understand that making mistakes is part of the growth process and each failure brings you closer to success. Adopt a growth mindset, where challenges are viewed as chances to improve and develop new skills.

Staying Motivated

Maintaining motivation throughout the implementation phase is crucial for sustained progress. One effective way to stay motivated is to keep your end goal in mind. Visualize the benefits and rewards of achieving your goal and how it will positively impact your life. This visualization can serve as a powerful motivator, especially during challenging times.

Set short-term milestones and celebrate your achievements along the way. These mini victories provide a sense of accomplishment and keep you motivated to continue. Rewards don't have to be extravagant; even small treats or breaks can boost your spirits and maintain enthusiasm.

Accountability is another key factor in staying motivated. Share your goals and progress with a trusted friend, family member, or mentor who can provide support and hold you accountable. Regular check-ins with your accountability partner can help you stay on track and address any challenges that arise.

Maintaining Momentum

Consistency is essential for maintaining momentum. Establish a routine that includes dedicated time for working on your tasks. Consistency builds habits, and once something becomes a habit, it requires less conscious effort to maintain. Whether it's setting aside time each morning to work on your goals or dedicating specific days of the week to certain tasks, a routine can help you stay focused and productive.

Track your progress regularly to ensure you're moving in the right direction. Use tools like journals, spreadsheets, or apps to monitor your achievements and identify any areas that need adjustment. Seeing tangible evidence of your progress can be incredibly motivating and reinforce your commitment to your goals.

Adaptability is also crucial for maintaining momentum. Life is unpredictable, and circumstances can change, requiring you to adjust your plans. Be flexible and willing to modify your action plan as needed. This adaptability ensures that you can continue making progress even when faced with unexpected challenges.

Overcoming Setbacks

Setbacks are a natural part of any journey. How you respond to them can significantly impact your progress. Instead of viewing setbacks as failures, see them as opportunities to learn and grow. Analyse what went wrong, identify the lessons learned, and apply these insights to your future efforts. This proactive approach helps you build resilience and improve your problem-solving skills.

When you encounter setbacks, practice self-compassion. Avoid harsh self-criticism and instead treat yourself with kindness and understanding. Acknowledge your efforts and remind yourself that setbacks are temporary and part of the process. Self-compassion helps you maintain a positive mindset and stay motivated to keep going.

Seeking Support

Don't hesitate to seek support when needed. Surround yourself with positive influences who can provide guidance, encouragement, and constructive feedback. Join groups or communities related to your goals where you can share experiences, gain insights, and find inspiration. Support networks can provide a sense of belonging and motivate you to persevere.

Implementing your action plan is a crucial step towards achieving your goals and building confidence. By taking the first steps, overcoming initial resistance, staying motivated, and maintaining momentum, you can turn your plans into reality. Every small action counts and brings you closer to your desired outcome. Stay flexible, seek support, and celebrate your progress along the way.

With determination and perseverance, you can achieve your goals and unlock your full potential.

7: *Monitoring and Adjusting Your Plan*

Once you've taken the initial steps to implement your action plan, the next crucial phase is to monitor and adjust your plan as needed. This dynamic approach ensures that you remain on track and can adapt to any changes or obstacles that may arise. In this section, we'll explore strategies for effectively monitoring your progress and making necessary adjustments to stay aligned with your goals.

Monitoring your progress is essential for maintaining momentum and ensuring that you're moving in the right direction. Regularly reviewing your tasks and deadlines allows you to track your achievements and identify any areas that may require additional focus or adjustment. One effective way to monitor your progress is to set aside dedicated time each week to review your action plan. During this review, assess what tasks you've completed, what's still pending, and any challenges you encountered.

Use tools like journals, spreadsheets, or digital apps to document your progress. These tools provide a visual representation of your accomplishments and help you stay organized. Checking off completed tasks provides a sense of accomplishment and motivates you to keep going. Additionally, maintaining a record of your progress allows you to reflect on your journey and appreciate how far you've come.

As you monitor your progress, it's important to remain flexible and open to making adjustments. Life is unpredictable, and circumstances can change, requiring you to adapt your plan. When you encounter obstacles or realize that certain tasks are taking longer than expected, don't be afraid to revise your deadlines and priorities. The key is to stay committed to your overall goal while being adaptable in your approach.

Adjusting your plan involves reassessing your tasks and deadlines to ensure they remain realistic and achievable. If you find that certain tasks are consistently being delayed, take a closer look to understand why. It could be due to a lack of resources, insufficient time, or unforeseen challenges. Once you identify the root cause, make the necessary adjustments to address the issue. This might involve reallocating resources, extending deadlines, or breaking tasks down into even smaller steps.

Seeking feedback from others can also be invaluable when monitoring and adjusting your plan. Share your progress with a trusted friend, family member, or mentor who can provide an outside perspective. They may offer insights and suggestions that you hadn't considered, helping you overcome obstacles and improve your approach. Regular check-ins with your accountability partner can also help you stay on track and motivated.

Another important aspect of monitoring and adjusting your plan is to celebrate your successes, no matter how small. Recognizing and rewarding yourself for your achievements reinforces positive behaviour and boosts your confidence. It's easy to get caught up in the pursuit of your goal and overlook the progress you've made along the way. Take time to acknowledge your hard work and dedication and use these moments of celebration to recharge and stay motivated.

Mindfulness and self-reflection are also crucial components of this process. Regularly take a step back to reflect on your journey, assessing what's working well and what could be improved. Mindfulness practices, such as meditation or journaling, can help you stay present and focused, allowing you to gain valuable insights into your thought patterns and behaviours. This self-awareness enables you to make more informed decisions and adjustments to your plan.

It's important to remember that setbacks and challenges are a natural part of any journey. When you encounter obstacles, view them as opportunities for growth and learning. Analyse what went wrong, identify the lessons learned, and apply these insights to your future efforts. This proactive approach helps you build resilience and improve your problem-solving skills.

Staying adaptable also means being open to new opportunities and ideas. As you progress, you may discover new strategies or resources that can enhance your plan. Don't be afraid to incorporate these new elements into your approach, even if it means deviating from your original plan. The ability to adapt and innovate is a valuable skill that can significantly contribute to your success.

Monitoring and adjusting your plan is a dynamic and ongoing process that ensures you stay on track and make consistent progress toward your goals. By regularly reviewing your tasks and deadlines, seeking feedback, celebrating successes, and remaining adaptable, you can navigate any challenges that arise and stay aligned with your objectives. The journey to achieving your goals is not always a straight path, but with dedication, flexibility, and resilience, you can overcome obstacles and achieve your desired outcomes.

Stay committed, stay motivated, and continue to adjust your plan as needed to reach your full potential.

Chapter 4: Building a Productive Routine

"Discover how to establish a daily routine that maximizes productivity. I'll share techniques for time management, creating a conducive work environment, and minimizing distractions.

A well-structured routine helps maintain consistency and momentum. Let's work together to build a routine that keeps you productive and focused."

Synopsis

In this section, we'll focus on creating a productive routine that supports your goals and fosters a sense of accomplishment. A well-structured routine can help you maintain consistency, stay motivated, and effectively manage your time. Let's dive into the key components of building a productive routine.

1: Understanding the Importance of a Routine

We'll explore why having a routine is crucial for productivity. We'll discuss the benefits of structure and consistency, including reduced stress, increased efficiency, and a greater sense of control over your day.

2: Identifying Your Most Productive Times

Everyone has different peak productivity times. Here, we'll help you identify when you are most alert and focused. We'll look at techniques to track your energy levels and maximize your most productive hours for the most important tasks.

3: Setting Priorities and Goals

Prioritization is key to a productive routine. This section will guide you in setting clear, actionable goals and prioritizing your tasks. We'll introduce tools like the Eisenhower Matrix and time-blocking to help you manage your to-do list effectively.

4: Creating a Daily Schedule

A daily schedule is the backbone of a productive routine. We'll walk through the steps of creating a balanced schedule that includes work, self-care, and leisure. This section will include tips on how to plan your day the night before and adjust your schedule as needed.

5: Incorporating Breaks and Downtime

Regular breaks are essential for maintaining productivity and avoiding burnout. We'll discuss the science behind taking breaks and provide strategies for incorporating short breaks and longer downtime into your routine.

6: Minimizing Distractions

Distractions can derail even the best-laid plans. In this section, we'll identify common distractions and offer practical tips to minimize them. From managing digital interruptions to creating a conducive work environment, we'll cover strategies to help you stay focused.

7: Establishing Morning and Evening Routines

Your morning and evening routines set the tone for your entire day. We'll explore how to create effective morning routines that energize you and evening routines that help you unwind and prepare for the next day.

8: Staying Flexible and Adapting Your Routine

Life is unpredictable, and sometimes your routine will need to adapt. We'll discuss the importance of flexibility and how to adjust your routine when circumstances change without losing momentum.

9: Reviewing and Refining Your Routine

A productive routine requires regular review and refinement. In this final section, we'll provide tips for evaluating your routine's effectiveness and adjusting keep it aligned with your goals and needs.

By the end of Building a Productive Routine, you'll have a comprehensive understanding of how to build and maintain a productive routine that supports your personal and professional goals.

A successful routine is one that works for you and evolves as you grow. Let's get started on creating a routine that helps you thrive.

1: Understanding the Importance of a Routine

Creating and maintaining a routine is a powerful tool for enhancing productivity and achieving your goals. A well-structured routine provides numerous benefits, including reduced stress, increased efficiency, and a greater sense of control over your day.

Here we'll explore why having a routine is crucial for productivity and how it can positively impact your life.

The Benefits of Structure and Consistency

One of the most significant advantages of having a routine is the structure and consistency it brings to your daily life. When you have a set routine, you know what to expect and what needs to be done at any given time. This predictability reduces the mental load of decision-making and helps you stay focused on your tasks. By establishing a consistent pattern, you can allocate time and energy more effectively, ensuring that important tasks are prioritized and completed.

Reduced Stress

A well-defined routine can significantly reduce stress by eliminating the uncertainty and chaos that often accompany an unstructured day. When you have a routine, you can anticipate what's coming next and prepare accordingly. This foresight allows you to manage your time better and reduces the likelihood of last-minute rushes or missed deadlines.

Furthermore, routines can incorporate self-care activities that promote relaxation and well-being. Whether it's a morning meditation, a regular exercise session, or a designated time for hobbies, these activities provide opportunities to unwind and recharge. Incorporating self-care into your routine helps you maintain a healthy work-life balance and reduces overall stress levels.

Increased Efficiency

Routines streamline your daily activities, making you more efficient and productive. By following a set schedule, you can minimize the time and energy spent on deciding what to do next. This efficiency frees up mental resources that can be redirected towards more important and creative tasks.

For example, consider your morning routine. If you consistently follow the same steps each day—waking up, brushing your teeth, having breakfast, and planning your day—you develop a rhythm that becomes second nature. This autopilot mode allows you to start your day smoothly and quickly, leaving you with more time and energy to focus on your priorities.

Greater Sense of Control

Having a routine gives you a greater sense of control over your day. When you plan and organize your activities, you can proactively manage your time and responsibilities. This control empowers you to make intentional choices about how you spend your time, rather than reacting to external demands and distractions.

A sense of control is essential for maintaining motivation and confidence. When you feel in control of your schedule, you're more likely to stay committed to your goals and take consistent action towards achieving them. This proactive approach helps you build momentum and maintain progress, even when faced with challenges or setbacks.

Implementing a Routine

To reap the benefits of a routine, it's important to create one that aligns with your goals, preferences, and lifestyle. Here are some steps to help you implement an effective routine:

1. Identify Your Priorities: Start by identifying your key priorities and goals. What activities are most important for your personal and professional growth? Consider your long-term objectives and the daily tasks that contribute to achieving them.

2. Create a Schedule: Based on your priorities, create a daily or weekly schedule that outlines your activities and tasks. Allocate specific time slots for each task, ensuring that you balance work, self-care, and leisure activities. Be realistic about the time required for each activity and avoid overloading your schedule.

3. Start Small: If you're new to routines, start with a few key activities and gradually build from there. Establishing a routine takes time and effort, so it's important to be patient and consistent. Focus on integrating one or two new habits at a time until they become part of your daily routine.

4. Be Flexible: While routines provide structure, it's important to remain flexible and adaptable. Life is unpredictable, and unexpected events can disrupt your schedule. Allow room for adjustments and be willing to modify your routine as needed.

Flexibility ensures that you can stay on track without becoming rigid or stressed.

5. Track Your Progress: Monitor your progress and reflect on how your routine is working for you. Are there any areas where you can improve efficiency or balance? Regularly reviewing your routine allows you to make necessary adjustments and optimize your schedule for better results.

6. Celebrate Successes: Acknowledge and celebrate your achievements, no matter how small. Recognizing your progress reinforces positive behaviour and motivates you to continue following your routine.

Celebrations can be simple, such as treating yourself to something you enjoy or taking a moment to appreciate your hard work.

Maintaining Your Routine

Maintaining a routine requires commitment and consistency. Here are some tips to help you stay on track:

Set Reminders: Use alarms, calendar notifications, or task management apps to remind you of your scheduled activities. Reminders help you stay accountable and ensure that you don't forget important tasks.

Find Accountability: Share your routine with a friend, family member, or mentor who can provide support and encouragement. Regular check-ins with an accountability partner can help you stay committed and address any challenges that arise.

Stay Motivated: Keep your motivation high by regularly reviewing your goals and reminding yourself of the benefits of your routine. Visualize the positive outcomes of your efforts and focus on the progress you're making.

Adapt as Needed: Life is dynamic, and your routine may need to evolve over time. Be open to making changes that enhance your productivity and well-being. Periodically reassess your routine and adjust ensure it continues to serve your needs.

Understanding the importance of a routine is essential for enhancing productivity and achieving your goals. By providing structure and consistency, reducing stress, increasing efficiency, and giving you a greater sense of control, a well-defined routine can significantly improve your daily life.

Implementing and maintaining a routine requires commitment, flexibility, and regular reflection, but the benefits are well worth the effort. Embrace the power of a routine and watch as it transforms your productivity and overall well-being.

2: Identifying Your Most Productive Times

Understanding when you are at your peak productivity can significantly enhance your efficiency and overall success. Everyone has different times of the day when they feel most alert, focused, and capable of tackling challenging tasks. Identifying these periods and aligning your schedule to take advantage of them can make a tremendous difference in your productivity and sense of accomplishment.

The Importance of Knowing Your Peak Times

Knowing your peak productivity times allows you to allocate your most demanding tasks to these periods, ensuring that you are working when your mind is at its sharpest. This not only increases the quality of your work but also helps you complete tasks more quickly and with less effort. Conversely, scheduling less demanding activities during your lower energy periods can prevent burnout and maintain a steady workflow throughout the day.

Techniques to Track Your Energy Levels

To identify your most productive times, start by tracking your energy levels throughout the day. Here are a few techniques to help you monitor and analyse your patterns:

1. Energy Logs: Keep a daily log of your energy levels at regular intervals, such as every hour. Rate your energy on a scale from 1 to 10 and note any significant fluctuations. This will help you see patterns over time.

2. Activity and Mood Journal: In addition to energy levels, track your mood and productivity. Note what tasks you are working on, how you feel about them, and how effectively you are completing them. Over a week or two, you will start to notice trends in your productivity and mood.

3. Apps and Tools: Use productivity and time-tracking apps like Toggl, RescueTime, or Clockify to monitor how you spend your time and when you are most productive. These tools can provide detailed reports and insights into your work habits.

4. Biological Rhythms: Pay attention to your natural biological rhythms. Many people experience peaks and

troughs in their energy levels that align with their circadian rhythms. Morning people, or "larks," often feel most energetic in the early hours, while "night owls" may hit their stride later in the day.

Analysing Your Patterns

After tracking your energy levels for a couple of weeks, review your data to identify your peak productivity periods. Look for consistent times when your energy levels are high, and your productivity is at its best. These are the times when you should aim to schedule your most important and demanding tasks.

Maximizing Your Productive Hours

Once you have identified your peak productivity times, it's important to make the most of them. Here are some strategies to help you maximize these hours:

1. Prioritize Important Tasks: Schedule your most critical and challenging tasks during your peak productivity periods. This ensures that you are tackling these tasks when you are most alert and capable, leading to better quality work and faster completion times.

2. Minimize Distractions: Protect your peak productivity times by minimizing distractions. Turn off notifications, close unnecessary tabs on your computer, and create a focused work environment. Inform colleagues or family members of your need for uninterrupted time.

3. Use Time Blocking: Allocate specific blocks of time for different types of work. For example, use your peak hours for deep work and important projects, and schedule routine

tasks or meetings for times when your energy levels are lower.

4. Take Regular Breaks: Even during your most productive times, it's important to take regular breaks to avoid burnout. Use techniques like the Pomodoro Technique, where you work for 25 minutes and then take a 5-minute break, to maintain focus and energy.

5. Listen to Your Body: Be flexible and responsive to your body's signals. If you notice a change in your energy patterns, adjust your schedule accordingly. Flexibility allows you to adapt to changes and maintain high productivity levels.

6. Stay Healthy: Maintaining a healthy lifestyle can significantly impact your energy levels and productivity. Ensure you get enough sleep, eat nutritious meals, stay hydrated, and exercise regularly. A healthy body supports a productive mind.

Identifying and leveraging your most productive times is a powerful strategy for enhancing your efficiency and achieving your goals. By tracking your energy levels, analysing your patterns, and scheduling your tasks accordingly, you can work smarter, not harder. Everyone's peak productivity times are different, so it's important to find what works best for you and create a schedule that aligns with your natural rhythms.

You can optimize your workday, reduce stress, and enjoy a greater sense of control and accomplishment.

3: Setting Priorities and Goals

Prioritization is the cornerstone of a productive routine, enabling you to focus on what truly matters and make meaningful progress toward your objectives. In this section, we'll explore how to set clear, actionable goals and effectively prioritize your tasks. By implementing practical tools like the Eisenhower Matrix and time-blocking, you can manage your to-do list with confidence and clarity.

The first step in setting priorities and goals is to understand what you truly want to achieve. Start by defining your long-term objectives, whether they are personal, professional, or a mix of both. Once you have a clear vision of your desired outcomes, break these larger goals into smaller, manageable tasks. This process not only makes your goals more attainable but also provides a clear roadmap to follow.

One effective tool, discussed in 'developing an action plan' earlier for prioritizing tasks is the Eisenhower Matrix, also known as the Urgent-Important Matrix. This method helps you categorize tasks based on their urgency and importance, allowing you to focus on what truly matters.

The matrix is divided into four quadrants:

1. Urgent and Important: Tasks that require immediate attention and are crucial to your goals. These should be your top priority.

2. Important but Not Urgent: Tasks that are essential but can be scheduled for later. These should be your next focus.

3. Urgent but Not Important: Tasks that require quick action but don't significantly impact your long-term goals. Delegate these if possible.

4. Not Urgent and Not Important: Tasks that have little impact on your overall goals. These should be minimized or eliminated.

By categorizing your tasks in this way, you can ensure that you are spending your time and energy on activities that align with your priorities and contribute to your long-term success.

Another powerful strategy for setting priorities is time-blocking. This technique involves dividing your day into blocks of time dedicated to specific tasks or activities. By allocating time slots for each task, you can create a structured schedule that helps you stay focused and avoid distractions. Time-blocking also allows you to balance different areas of your life, ensuring that you dedicate time to work, self-care, and leisure.

When setting goals, it's important to make them SMART: Specific, Measurable, Achievable, Relevant, and Time-bound. We talked through this earlier in 'understanding the importance of clear goals' but it's always a good idea to go over things more than once. This framework ensures that your goals are clear and attainable, providing a solid foundation for your action plan.

For example, instead of setting a vague goal like "get fit," a SMART goal would be "exercise for 30 minutes, five times a week, for the next three months." This specific and measurable goal gives you a clear target to aim for and track your progress.

Regularly reviewing and adjusting your priorities is essential for staying on track. Life is dynamic, and circumstances can change, requiring you to adapt your plans. Set aside time each week to reflect on your progress, assess your current priorities, and make any necessary adjustments. This practice ensures that you remain aligned with your goals and can respond effectively to new challenges or opportunities.

Celebrate your achievements along the way. Recognizing and rewarding your progress, no matter how small, reinforces positive behaviour and motivates you to continue striving toward your goals. Celebrations can be as simple as treating yourself to something you enjoy or taking a moment to appreciate your hard work.

By setting clear, actionable goals and prioritizing your tasks effectively, you can create a productive routine that supports your personal and professional growth. Implementing tools like the Eisenhower Matrix and time-blocking will help you manage your to-do list with confidence, allowing you to focus on what truly matters and make meaningful progress toward your objectives.

4: Creating a Daily Schedule

A daily schedule is the backbone of a productive routine, providing structure and direction to your day. By planning your activities in advance, you can ensure a balanced approach that includes work, self-care, and leisure. In this section, we'll walk through the steps of creating a balanced schedule, including tips on how to plan your day the night before and adjust your schedule as needed.

The first step in creating a daily schedule is to identify your key priorities and tasks for the day. Start by reviewing your long-term goals and breaking them down into actionable steps. Determine what needs to be accomplished each day to stay on track and make consistent progress. This practice ensures that your daily activities align with your overall objectives and contribute to your long-term success.

Once you have a clear list of tasks, allocate specific time slots for each activity. This technique, known as time-blocking, helps you create a structured schedule that maximizes productivity and minimizes distractions. Begin by designating blocks of time for your most important tasks, typically during your peak productivity periods. Then, schedule time for routine tasks, meetings, and other commitments. Be sure to include breaks and buffer time to accommodate unexpected interruptions or delays.

Planning your day the night before is a powerful strategy for staying organized and focused. Take a few minutes each evening to review your goals and priorities for the next day. Create a to-do list and allocate time slots for each task. This practice not only helps you start the day with a clear plan but also reduces morning stress and decision fatigue.

It's important to maintain a balance between work, self-care, and leisure in your daily schedule. Allocate time for activities that nourish your mind, body, and spirit, such as exercise, meditation, hobbies, and social interactions. A well-rounded schedule promotes overall well-being and prevents burnout, allowing you to sustain high levels of productivity and motivation.

Flexibility is key to a successful daily schedule. Life is unpredictable, and circumstances can change, requiring you to adapt your plans. Be prepared to adjust your schedule as needed to accommodate new priorities or unexpected events.

This flexibility ensures that you remain productive without becoming rigid or stressed.

Regularly reviewing and adjusting your schedule is essential for maintaining its effectiveness. Set aside time each week to reflect on your progress, assess your current schedule, and make any necessary adjustments. This practice ensures that your daily routine remains aligned with your goals and can respond effectively to new challenges or opportunities.

By creating a balanced and flexible daily schedule, you can establish a productive routine that supports your personal and professional growth. Planning your day the night before and incorporating time-blocking techniques will help you stay organized and focused, allowing you to make the most of each day and achieve your goals with confidence.

5: Incorporating Breaks and Downtime

Incorporating regular breaks and downtime into your daily routine is crucial for maintaining productivity and avoiding burnout. While it might seem counterintuitive, taking breaks can enhance your efficiency and overall performance. This section will delve into the science behind taking breaks and provide strategies for integrating short breaks and longer periods of rest into your routine.

The human brain is not designed to focus on tasks for prolonged periods without rest. Research has shown that working for extended hours without breaks leads to diminished returns, as fatigue sets in and cognitive function declines. By taking regular breaks, you give your brain the opportunity to rest and recharge, improving your ability to concentrate and process information when you return to work.

One popular method for incorporating breaks into your routine is the Pomodoro Technique. This technique involves working for a set period, typically 25 minutes, followed by a short break of 5 minutes. After completing four work intervals, or "Pomodoros," you take a longer break of 15-30 minutes. This structured approach helps maintain focus and productivity while preventing burnout. The frequent breaks allow you to refresh your mind and maintain a high level of performance throughout the day.

Another important aspect of incorporating breaks is recognizing the need for longer periods of downtime. While short breaks help maintain daily productivity, extended periods of rest are essential for overall well-being and preventing long-term burnout. Schedule regular downtime, such as weekends or vacations, to disconnect from work and recharge. During these periods, engage in activities that you enjoy and that help you relax, such as spending time with loved ones, pursuing hobbies, or simply resting.

Mindfulness and relaxation techniques can also be beneficial during breaks. Practices such as deep breathing, meditation, or a short walk can help clear your mind and reduce stress. These activities not only provide a mental break but also contribute to your overall well-being by reducing anxiety and promoting a sense of calm.

Physical movement is another effective way to refresh your mind during breaks. Incorporating short stretches or a quick exercise routine can boost your energy levels and improve your focus. Physical activity increases blood flow to the brain, enhancing cognitive function and creativity. Whether it's a brief walk outside or a few minutes of stretching at your desk, moving your body during breaks can significantly impact your productivity and well-being.

It's also important to create a work environment that supports regular breaks. Set reminders to take breaks and ensure that your workspace is conducive to relaxation. This might mean having a comfortable chair for stretching or a designated area where you can step away from your desk. Encouraging a culture of regular breaks within your team or organization can also promote collective well-being and productivity.

Ultimately, the key to incorporating breaks and downtime is to listen to your body and mind. Pay attention to signs of fatigue and take breaks as needed. Taking care of your mental and physical health is essential for sustaining long-term productivity and achieving your goals.

6: Minimizing Distractions

Distractions can derail even the best-laid plans, making it challenging to stay focused and productive. In this section, we'll identify common distractions and offer practical tips to minimize them. From managing digital interruptions to creating a conducive work environment, we'll cover strategies to help you stay focused.

One of the most common sources of distraction in today's digital age is technology. Constant notifications from emails, social media, and messaging apps can interrupt your workflow and reduce your efficiency. To minimize digital distractions, start by turning off non-essential notifications during work hours. Set specific times to check your emails and social media, rather than allowing them to interrupt you throughout the day. Using apps or browser extensions that block distracting websites during work periods can also help you stay focused.

Creating a conducive work environment is another crucial step in minimizing distractions. Designate a specific area for work that is free from distractions and conducive to concentration. Ensure that your workspace is organized and clutter-free, as a tidy environment can enhance focus and reduce stress. If you work from home, communicate with family members or housemates about your need for uninterrupted work time, setting clear boundaries and expectations.

Managing auditory distractions is also important for maintaining focus. If you work in a noisy environment, consider using noise-cancelling headphones or playing background music that helps you concentrate. Some people find that ambient noise or classical music can enhance their focus, while others prefer complete silence. Experiment with different soundscapes to determine what works best for you.

Another effective strategy for minimizing distractions is time-blocking. By allocating specific blocks of time for focused work, meetings, and breaks, you can create a structured schedule that reduces the likelihood of interruptions. During your designated work blocks, commit to focusing solely on your tasks, and avoid multitasking, as it can lead to decreased productivity and increased errors.

It's also essential to address internal distractions, such as wandering thoughts or daydreaming. Practicing mindfulness can help you stay present and focused on the task at hand. Techniques such as deep breathing, meditation, or grounding exercises can help you regain focus when your mind starts to wander. Regularly reminding yourself of your goals and the reasons behind your tasks can also help you stay motivated and engaged.

Setting clear goals and priorities can further help you stay focused and minimize distractions. When you have a clear plan and know what you need to accomplish, it's easier to stay on track and avoid getting sidetracked by less important tasks. Break down your goals into smaller, manageable steps, and tackle them one at a time, celebrating your progress along the way.

Take care of your physical and mental well-being. Ensure that you get enough sleep, eat nutritious meals, and stay hydrated. Physical exercise can also boost your focus and energy levels. When you feel good physically, it's easier to stay focused and productive.

By implementing these strategies, you can minimize distractions and create an environment that supports sustained focus and productivity. Minimizing distractions is an ongoing process, and it may take time to find the methods that work best for you.

Stay patient and committed to creating a distraction-free work environment, and you'll be well on your way to achieving your goals.

7: Establishing Morning and Evening Routines

Your morning and evening routines are crucial for setting the tone for your entire day. These routines help you start your day with energy and purpose, and wind down in the evening to ensure a restful night and a fresh start the next day. Establishing effective morning and evening routines can enhance your productivity, well-being, and overall sense of control.

A well-structured morning routine is essential for beginning your day on a positive note. How you start your day can significantly impact your mood, energy levels, and productivity. Begin by waking up at a consistent time each day, allowing your body to establish a natural rhythm. This consistency helps regulate your internal clock, leading to better sleep and increased daytime energy.

Starting your morning with a few minutes of mindfulness can set a calm and focused tone for the day. Whether it's meditation, deep breathing, or simply sitting in silence, taking time to centre yourself can help reduce stress and improve your mental clarity. Consider writing in a gratitude journal to reflect on the positive aspects of your life, fostering a sense of appreciation and optimism.

Incorporating physical activity into your morning routine can also boost your energy and mood. Exercise releases endorphins, which enhance your mood and provide a natural energy boost. Whether it's a brisk walk, yoga, or a more intense workout, find an activity that you enjoy and can commit to regularly. Even a short 10-minute session can make a significant difference in how you feel throughout the day.

Nutrition plays a vital role in your morning routine. Starting your day with a healthy, balanced breakfast fuels your body and mind. Aim for a combination of protein, healthy fats, and complex carbohydrates to provide sustained energy. Avoid high-sugar foods that can lead to energy crashes later in the day. Hydration is equally important; drinking a glass of water first thing in the morning can kickstart your metabolism and help you stay alert.

Planning your day in the morning can help you feel organized and in control. Take a few minutes to review your goals and priorities and create a to-do list. Time-blocking your tasks can provide structure and ensure that you allocate time for both important work and breaks. This practice helps you stay focused and reduces the likelihood of feeling overwhelmed.

As the day comes to an end, an effective evening routine is essential for unwinding and preparing for restful sleep. A consistent evening routine signals to your body that it's time to wind down, making it easier to fall asleep and enjoy restorative rest. Start by setting a consistent bedtime to regulate your sleep cycle. Aim for 7-9 hours of sleep per night, as adequate rest is crucial for cognitive function, mood, and overall health.

Begin your evening routine by disconnecting from electronic devices at least an hour before bed. The blue light emitted by screens can interfere with the production of melatonin, the hormone that regulates sleep. Instead, engage in relaxing activities such as reading, journaling, or taking a warm bath. These activities help calm your mind and body, preparing you for sleep.

Reflecting on your day can be a valuable part of your evening routine. Spend a few minutes journaling about your experiences, achievements, and any challenges you faced. This practice can help you process your thoughts and emotions, providing a sense of closure for the day. Additionally, writing down any tasks or ideas for the next day can help clear your mind and reduce anxiety about unfinished business.

Incorporating relaxation techniques into your evening routine can promote better sleep. Deep breathing exercises, progressive muscle relaxation, or gentle stretching can help release tension and prepare your body for rest. Consider listening to calming music or guided meditations to create a soothing atmosphere.

Preparing for the next day in the evening can also set you up for success. Lay out your clothes, pack your bag, and prepare your lunch if needed. This preparation reduces decision-making in the morning and allows you to start your day smoothly. Reviewing your schedule and to-do list for the next day can also provide a sense of readiness and reduce morning stress.

Creating a bedtime ritual can further enhance your evening routine. Engage in activities that signal to your body that it's time to sleep, such as dimming the lights, brushing your teeth, and setting a comfortable sleep environment. Ensure that your bedroom is cool, dark, and quiet, as these conditions are conducive to restful sleep.

Establishing effective morning and evening routines is a personal process. What works for one person may not work for another. Experiment with different activities and schedules to find what best suits your lifestyle and preferences. The key is consistency; once you find a routine that works, stick to it to reap the benefits over time.

Incorporating these practices into your daily life can help you feel more energized, focused, and in control. By starting your day with intention and ending it with relaxation, you create a balanced approach that supports your overall well-being and productivity.

Establishing morning and evening routines is a powerful way to enhance your confidence and achieve your goals, one day at a time.

8: Staying Flexible and Adapting Your Routine

Life is inherently unpredictable, and even the most well-crafted routines can be disrupted by unforeseen circumstances. Whether it's an unexpected work project, a family emergency, or a sudden change in your personal life, the ability to stay flexible and adapt your routine is essential for maintaining productivity and achieving your goals. In this chapter, we'll explore the importance of flexibility and provide strategies for adjusting your routine when circumstances change, all without losing momentum.

The Importance of Flexibility

Flexibility is a crucial aspect of any effective routine. While having a structured plan can provide direction and help you stay on track, rigidity can lead to frustration and burnout when things don't go as planned. Embracing flexibility allows you to navigate life's ups and downs with greater ease, ensuring that you can continue to make progress even in the face of challenges.

Being flexible doesn't mean abandoning your routine altogether. Instead, it means being willing to adjust your plans and priorities as needed. This adaptability can help you stay resilient and maintain a positive mindset, which are key components of long-term success.

Strategies for Staying Flexible

1. Prioritize Your Core Tasks: Identify the most important tasks that must be completed, regardless of any changes in your schedule. By focusing on these core tasks, you can ensure that you continue to make progress on your most critical goals. This might mean temporarily postponing less important activities or finding more efficient ways to complete them.

2. Embrace the Power of Time-Blocking: Time-blocking is a powerful tool for staying organized and focused. When circumstances change, adjust your time blocks to accommodate new priorities. For example, if you need to take care of an urgent task, shift your schedule to allocate time for it without sacrificing your most important activities. This approach allows you to remain productive while being responsive to changing demands.

3. Build Buffer Time into Your Schedule: Incorporating buffer time into your routine can provide a cushion for unexpected events. Schedule short breaks between tasks and allocate time for unforeseen activities. This buffer time can help you manage disruptions without feeling overwhelmed or falling behind on your work.

4. Stay Mindful and Present: Practicing mindfulness can help you stay grounded and focused, even when your routine is disrupted. Take a few moments each day to breathe deeply, centre yourself, and reflect on your priorities. This practice can help you maintain a sense of calm and clarity, enabling you to adapt more effectively to changing circumstances.

5. Communicate and Delegate: When unexpected events arise, communicate with those around you and delegate tasks if possible. Whether it's asking a colleague to cover for you at work or seeking support from family members, effective communication and delegation can help you manage your responsibilities more efficiently.

Adjusting Your Routine

When you need to adjust your routine, it's important to do so thoughtfully and intentionally. Here are some steps to help you make effective adjustments:

1. Assess the Situation: Take a moment to assess the new circumstances and determine how they impact your routine. Identify any immediate actions that need to be taken and consider the potential long-term effects on your schedule.

2. Reevaluate Your Priorities: With the new information in mind, reevaluate your priorities and determine which tasks

are most important. Focus on activities that align with your core goals and adjust your schedule accordingly.

3. Create a Revised Plan: Develop a revised plan that incorporates the necessary changes. Use time-blocking to allocate time for new tasks and ensure that you continue to make progress on your most important activities. Remember to include buffer time and breaks to help you manage any additional disruptions.

4. Stay Flexible and Open-Minded: Remain open to further adjustments as needed. Flexibility is an ongoing process, and being willing to adapt your routine as circumstances evolve can help you stay resilient and productive.

5. Reflect and Learn: After navigating a disruption, take time to reflect on the experience and identify any lessons learned. Consider how you can apply these insights to improve your routine and enhance your flexibility in the future.

Maintaining Momentum

While adjusting your routine is important, it's equally crucial to maintain momentum and continue making progress toward your goals. Here are some tips to help you stay motivated and focused:

1. Set Short-Term Goals: Break your larger goals into smaller, manageable steps. Setting short-term goals can help you stay focused and motivated, even when your routine is disrupted. Celebrate your progress and use these achievements to build momentum.

2. Stay Connected to Your Why: Remind yourself of the reasons behind your goals and the benefits of achieving them. Staying connected to your purpose can provide

motivation and drive, helping you stay committed to your routine even in challenging times.

3. Practice Self-Compassion: Be kind to yourself and recognize that disruptions are a normal part of life. Practice self-compassion and give yourself grace when things don't go as planned. This mindset can help you stay resilient and maintain a positive outlook.

4. Seek Support: Surround yourself with a supportive network of friends, family, and colleagues. Share your challenges and successes with them and seek their encouragement and advice. A strong support system can provide valuable perspective and motivation.

5. Focus on Progress, Not Perfection: Aim for progress rather than perfection. Recognize that setbacks and disruptions are part of the journey and focus on the steps you can take to move forward. Celebrate your efforts and the progress you make, no matter how small.

By staying flexible and adapting your routine, you can navigate life's uncertainties while continuing to make progress toward your goals. Embracing flexibility allows you to remain resilient, maintain momentum, and achieve success even in the face of challenges.

The key to long-term success is not a rigid routine but a dynamic and adaptable approach that supports your personal and professional growth.

Chapter 5: Overcoming Self-Doubt

"This chapter explores strategies to combat self-doubt and build self-confidence. It will guide you through exercises to identify and challenge negative self-talk, develop a positive mindset, and celebrate small wins.

Building confidence is crucial for sustaining progress and overcoming procrastination. Let's work together to strengthen your confidence and keep you moving forward."

Synopsis

Here we'll tackle the pervasive issue of self-doubt and how it can hinder your progress and fulfilment. Understanding and overcoming self-doubt is essential for building confidence and unlocking your true potential. Together, we'll explore strategies to silence your inner critic and cultivate a positive self-image.

Recognizing Self-Doubt

The first step in overcoming self-doubt is recognizing its presence. We'll discuss the common signs of self-doubt and how it manifests in your thoughts and behaviours. By identifying these patterns, you can begin to address and challenge them.

Challenging Negative Self-Talk

Negative self-talk is a major contributor to self-doubt. Here, we'll introduce techniques to identify and challenge your inner critic. We'll practice reframing negative thoughts into positive affirmations and constructive self dialogue.

Building Self-Compassion

Cultivating self-compassion is crucial for overcoming self-doubt. We'll discuss the importance of being kind to yourself and offer exercises to practice self-compassion. By treating yourself with the same kindness you extend to others, you can foster a healthier self-image.

Setting Realistic Expectations

Unrealistic expectations can fuel self-doubt. In this section, we'll explore how to set realistic and achievable goals. We'll discuss the importance of celebrating progress rather than perfection and recognizing your achievements along the way.

Seeking Support and Feedback

You don't have to battle self-doubt alone. We'll talk about the importance of seeking support from trusted friends, mentors, and professionals. Constructive feedback can help you gain perspective and validate your strengths.

Taking Small Steps

Overcoming self-doubt requires action. We'll emphasize the importance of taking small, manageable steps towards your goals. Each small success builds confidence and proves to yourself that you are capable and competent.

Reflecting on Your Journey

Regular reflection helps you see how far you've come and reinforces your progress. We'll provide tips for journaling and self-assessment to track your growth and maintain a positive outlook. Reflecting on your journey helps you stay motivated and confident.

The purpose of this chapter is to give you a deeper understanding of self-doubt and practical strategies to overcome it. Remember, self-doubt is a common experience, but it doesn't have to control your life. With patience, self-compassion, and perseverance, you can silence your inner critic and embrace your true potential. Together we can build a foundation of confidence and self-belief that will support you on your journey to success.

1: Recognizing Self-Doubt

Self-doubt can be a pervasive and debilitating force, often lurking in the background of our thoughts and subtly influencing our behaviours. It can erode confidence, hinder personal and professional growth, and prevent us from taking risks or pursuing our goals. The first step in overcoming self-doubt is recognizing its presence. By understanding the common signs and manifestations of self-doubt, you can begin to address and challenge these patterns, paving the way for greater self-assurance and success.

Self-doubt often manifests in negative self-talk. This internal dialogue can be harsh and critical, constantly questioning your abilities, decisions, and worth. You might find yourself thinking, "I'm not good enough," "I can't do this," or "What if I fail?" These thoughts can become a constant background noise, shaping your perception of yourself and your capabilities. Recognizing this negative self-talk is crucial, as it forms the foundation of self-doubt. Pay attention to your inner voice and the language it uses. Are you being overly critical or dismissive of your achievements? Identifying these patterns is the first step towards changing them.

Another common sign of self-doubt is procrastination. When you doubt your abilities, you might delay starting tasks or projects because you're afraid of failing or not meeting your own or others' expectations. Procrastination becomes a way to avoid confronting these fears. You might convince yourself that you'll do it later when you're "more prepared" or "more capable," but these delays only reinforce the cycle of self-doubt. By acknowledging procrastination as a symptom of self-doubt, you can begin to address the underlying fears and take steps towards breaking the cycle.

Perfectionism is another behaviour closely linked to self-doubt. The desire to be perfect in everything you do can stem from a fear of making mistakes or being judged. Perfectionists set unrealistically high standards for themselves and are often their own harshest critics. They might spend excessive amounts of time on tasks, constantly revising and tweaking, because they never feel their work is good enough. This pursuit of perfection can be paralyzing and prevent you from moving forward. Recognizing perfectionism as a manifestation of self-doubt allows you to challenge these unrealistic standards and adopt a more balanced perspective.

Self-doubt can also lead to avoidance behaviours. You might avoid taking on new challenges or opportunities because you're afraid of failing or being exposed as inadequate. This can manifest in various ways, such as declining a promotion, not applying for a job you're interested in, or avoiding social situations where you might be judged. These avoidance behaviours can limit your growth and reinforce feelings of inadequacy. By identifying these patterns, you can start to push yourself out of your comfort zone and build confidence through new experiences.

Seeking Validation

Another subtle but significant manifestation of self-doubt is the need for constant reassurance. You might find yourself seeking validation from others, needing them to confirm that you're making the right decisions or that you're capable. While it's natural to seek support from those around us, excessive reliance on external validation can indicate a lack of self-trust. Recognizing this need for reassurance can help you start to build your own self-confidence and trust in your abilities.

Imposter syndrome is a specific form of self-doubt that many people experience, especially high achievers. It's the feeling that you're not truly competent or deserving of your accomplishments and that at any moment, you'll be exposed as a fraud. Imposter syndrome can cause significant anxiety and prevent you from fully embracing your successes. If you find yourself discounting your achievements or attributing them to luck rather than your skills and effort, you might be experiencing imposter syndrome. Acknowledging this can be the first step towards combating these feelings and recognizing your true worth.

Physical manifestations of self-doubt can also be telling. You might notice increased stress, anxiety, or even physical symptoms like headaches, fatigue, or difficulty sleeping. These symptoms can be your body's way of signalling that you're struggling with self-doubt. By paying attention to these signs, you can start to address the root cause and take steps towards improving your mental and physical well-being.

Recognizing self-doubt is not about being harsh on yourself but about developing self-awareness. It's about acknowledging that self-doubt is a part of the human experience and that everyone faces it at some point. By bringing these patterns to light, you can begin to challenge and change them. Start by questioning the validity of your negative thoughts. Are they based on facts or assumptions? Would you say the same things to a friend in a similar situation? Often, we are much kinder and more supportive to others than we are to ourselves.

Practicing self-compassion is a powerful tool in overcoming self-doubt. Treat yourself with the same kindness and understanding you would offer to a friend. Recognize that making mistakes and facing challenges are part of the growth process and that they do not diminish your worth or capabilities.

Seeking support from others can also be beneficial. Talk to friends, family members, or a therapist about your feelings of self-doubt. They can offer perspective, encouragement, and practical advice. Sometimes, just voicing your doubts can help reduce their power over you.

Recognizing self-doubt is the first step towards overcoming it. By identifying the signs and manifestations of self-doubt in your thoughts and behaviours, you can begin to address and challenge these patterns. Developing self-awareness, practicing self-compassion, and seeking support are essential strategies in building confidence and moving past self-doubt.

Overcoming self-doubt is a journey, and each step you take brings you closer to a more confident and empowered version of yourself.

2: Challenging Negative Self-Talk

Negative self-talk is an insidious force that undermines our confidence and fuels self-doubt. It is that inner voice that criticizes, belittles, and casts doubt on our abilities and worth. To truly embrace overcoming self-doubt empowering self-esteem, it is essential to recognize and challenge this negative self-talk. By learning to identify the inner critic and reframing negative thoughts into positive affirmations and constructive self-dialogue, we can transform our mindset and bolster our self-esteem.

Identify

The first step in overcoming negative self-talk is to become aware of it. Often, these thoughts run on autopilot, ingrained in our subconscious and shaping our perceptions without our conscious awareness. Start by paying attention to your internal dialogue, especially in moments of stress, failure, or uncertainty. Notice the language you use with yourself. Are you compassionate and supportive, or do you quickly jump to criticism and self-blame? Common negative self-talk includes statements like "I'm not good enough," "I always mess up," or "I'll never succeed."

Challenge

Once you've identified these negative thoughts, the next step is to challenge them. Negative self-talk thrives on unquestioned acceptance, so it's crucial to critically examine the validity of these thoughts. Ask yourself: Is this thought based on fact or assumption? What evidence do I have to support or refute it? Would I say this to a friend or loved one? Often, you'll find that negative self-talk is rooted in irrational fears and unrealistic standards rather than objective reality.

Reframe

After challenging the negative thoughts, practice reframing them into positive affirmations. This doesn't mean simply replacing a negative thought with an overly optimistic one, but rather finding a balanced and constructive perspective. For example, if you catch yourself thinking, "I'll never get this right," reframe it to, "This is challenging, but with practice, I can improve." This shift in perspective acknowledges the difficulty while emphasizing your ability to grow and learn.

Positive affirmations are powerful tools in reshaping your internal dialogue. They help to reinforce a positive self-image and cultivate a mindset of self-compassion and resilience. Create a list of affirmations that resonate with you, focusing on your strengths, achievements, and potential. For instance, "I am capable and strong," "I learn from my mistakes," and "I am worthy of success and happiness." Repeat these affirmations daily, especially during moments of doubt, to reinforce a positive and empowering narrative.

Another effective technique is to practice constructive self-dialogue. This involves engaging in a more balanced and supportive conversation with yourself. When faced with a setback or challenge, instead of succumbing to harsh self-criticism, approach the situation with curiosity and kindness. Ask yourself questions like, "What can I learn from this experience?" or "How can I approach this differently next time?" This shift from judgment to curiosity fosters a growth mindset and encourages self-improvement rather than self-deprecation.

Mindfulness and meditation can also play a significant role in managing negative self-talk. By cultivating present-moment awareness, you can observe your thoughts without attachment or judgment. This practice helps to create distance between you and your negative thoughts, allowing you to see them for what they are – transient and often untrue mental events. Mindfulness can help you to respond to negative self-talk with greater clarity and composure, rather than being swept away by it.

It's important to recognize that challenging negative self-talk is not about suppressing or denying difficult emotions. Instead, it's about creating a compassionate and realistic internal environment where you can acknowledge your feelings without letting them define you. Emotions like fear, frustration, and disappointment are natural and valid, but they don't have to dictate your self-worth or capabilities. By practicing self-compassion, you can hold space for these emotions while still affirming your value and potential.

Building a support system can also aid in challenging negative self-talk. Surround yourself with people who uplift and encourage you. Share your struggles and successes with trusted friends, family, or mentors who can offer perspective and validation. Sometimes, hearing an external voice of reason can help to counteract the internal critic. Additionally, consider seeking the guidance of a therapist or counsellor who can provide professional support and strategies for managing negative self-talk.

Transforming your internal dialogue is a gradual process. It takes time, practice, and patience to shift deeply ingrained thought patterns. Celebrate your progress, no matter how small, and be gentle with yourself during setbacks. The goal is not to achieve perfect positivity but to cultivate a more balanced and supportive internal narrative.

Challenging negative self-talk involves several key steps: becoming aware of your internal dialogue, questioning the validity of negative thoughts, reframing them into positive affirmations, practicing constructive self-dialogue, incorporating mindfulness, and building a supportive network. By actively engaging in these practices, you can weaken the grip of the inner critic and foster a more empowering and resilient mindset.

This transformation is essential for building and maintaining confidence, enabling you to take decisive action towards your goals with a sense of self-assuredness and optimism.

3: Building Self-Compassion

Self-compassion is the practice of treating yourself with the same kindness, care, and understanding that you would offer to a good friend. It involves recognizing your own suffering, being gentle with yourself in moments of difficulty, and understanding that making mistakes and experiencing setbacks is part of the shared human experience. Cultivating self-compassion is crucial for overcoming self-doubt and fostering a healthier self-image.

At its core, self-compassion is about acknowledging your imperfections and responding to them with kindness and empathy, rather than judgment and criticism. It's about recognizing that you are not alone in your struggles and that others experience similar challenges. This understanding can help you feel more connected to others and less isolated in your difficulties.

Practicing self-compassion can have profound effects on your mental and emotional well-being. When you are kind to yourself, you are more likely to be resilient in the face of challenges and to recover more quickly from setbacks. Self-compassion helps to reduce feelings of shame and self-criticism, which are often at the root of self-doubt and insecurity. By being compassionate towards yourself, you can foster a more positive and accepting self-image.

Exercises to Practice Self-Compassion

1. Mindful Self-Awareness: The first step in cultivating self-compassion is becoming aware of your inner dialogue. Pay attention to the way you speak to yourself, especially in moments of failure or difficulty. Notice if your self-talk is harsh or critical and make a conscious effort to soften your tone. Mindfulness can help you become more aware of your thoughts and feelings without judgment.

2. Self-Compassionate Letter: Write a letter to yourself from the perspective of a compassionate friend. Imagine what they would say to you in a moment of struggle or failure. This exercise can help you to reframe your thoughts and to view yourself with more kindness and understanding.

3. Self-Soothing Activities: Engage in activities that bring you comfort and joy. This could be anything from taking a warm bath, listening to your favourite music, or spending

time in nature. These activities can help to nurture your emotional well-being and remind you that you deserve care and kindness.

4. Positive Affirmations: Use affirmations to reinforce positive self-talk and to challenge negative beliefs about yourself. For example, you might say to yourself, "I am worthy of love and compassion," or "I am doing my best, and that is enough." Repeat these affirmations regularly to help shift your mindset towards one of self-compassion.

5. Common Humanity: Remind yourself that you are not alone in your struggles. Everyone experiences difficulties and makes mistakes. Recognizing this common humanity can help you to feel more connected to others and less isolated in your experiences.

The Impact of Self-Compassion on Self-Doubt

Self-doubt often stems from a fear of not being good enough or from a tendency to compare yourself unfavourably to others. When you practice self-compassion, you are less likely to engage in these negative comparisons and more likely to appreciate your own unique strengths and qualities. Self-compassion allows you to acknowledge your mistakes without letting them define you, which can help to build confidence and resilience.

By treating yourself with kindness and understanding, you can create a more supportive and nurturing inner environment. This can help you to face challenges with greater courage and to take risks without fear of failure. Self-compassion can also enhance your relationships with others, as it allows you to be more empathetic and understanding towards their struggles as well.

Practical Tips for Cultivating Self-Compassion

Set Boundaries: Protect your time and energy by setting boundaries with others. This can help you to prioritize your own needs and to avoid overcommitting yourself.

Practice Gratitude: Take time each day to reflect on the things you are grateful for. This can help to shift your focus away from what you lack and towards what you have, fostering a sense of contentment and appreciation.

Seek Support: Surround yourself with people who are supportive and understanding. Talking to a trusted friend or therapist can help you to gain perspective and to feel less alone in your struggles.

Be Patient with Yourself: Change takes time, and it's important to be patient with yourself as you work on cultivating self-compassion. Recognize that it's a journey and that it's okay to take small steps towards your goals.

By incorporating these practices into your daily life, you can begin to develop a more compassionate and supportive relationship with yourself. This can help you to overcome self-doubt, to build resilience, and to move forward with greater confidence and ease.

Self-compassion is not about being perfect; it's about being kind to yourself amid imperfection.

4: Setting Realistic Expectations

Setting realistic expectations is a crucial step in building confidence and overcoming self-doubt. When you set unrealistic goals, you're more likely to feel overwhelmed and discouraged when you don't meet them. This, in turn, can fuel self-doubt and make it harder to stay motivated. On the other hand, setting realistic and achievable goals allows you to experience success, build confidence, and maintain momentum.

One of the first steps in setting realistic expectations is to understand your current abilities and limitations. This requires an honest assessment of your skills, resources, and available time. It's important to be kind to yourself during this process and recognize that everyone has limitations. By acknowledging these limitations, you can set goals that are challenging yet attainable, rather than setting yourself up for failure.

Take Small Steps

Next, break down your larger goals into smaller, manageable tasks. This not only makes the process less daunting but also allows you to track your progress and celebrate small victories along the way. For example, if your goal is to write a book, break it down into smaller tasks such as outlining the chapters, writing a certain number of words each day, and editing each section. By focusing on these smaller tasks, you can make steady progress towards your larger goal without feeling overwhelmed.

Another key aspect of setting realistic expectations is to be flexible and adaptable. Life is unpredictable, and things don't always go as planned. It's important to be willing to adjust your goals and expectations as needed, rather than rigidly sticking to a plan that may no longer be feasible. This flexibility allows you to stay motivated and continue making progress, even when faced with obstacles.

In addition to setting realistic goals, it's also important to celebrate your progress and achievements along the way. Many people fall into the trap of focusing solely on the end goal, neglecting to acknowledge the small steps they have taken to get there. By celebrating these small victories, you can build confidence and maintain motivation. This could be as simple as acknowledging your progress at the end of each day or treating yourself to a reward when you reach a milestone.

Progress Not Perfection

It's also important to recognize that perfection is not the goal. Perfectionism can be a major barrier to setting realistic expectations and achieving your goals. When you strive for perfection, you're more likely to become discouraged when things don't go exactly as planned. Instead, focus on making progress and doing your best, rather than striving for an unattainable ideal.

One way to combat perfectionism is to practice self-compassion. Be kind to yourself when you make mistakes or fall short of your goals. Remember that everyone makes mistakes and that setbacks are a natural part of the learning process. By treating yourself with the same kindness and understanding that you would offer to a friend, you can build resilience and maintain a positive outlook.

It's also helpful to surround yourself with supportive people who encourage you and celebrate your progress. This could be friends, family members, or a support group. Having a support system can provide motivation, accountability, and encouragement when you need it most.

It's important to regularly review and adjust your goals and expectations. As you make progress, your abilities and circumstances may change. Regularly reassessing your goals allows you to stay aligned with your current situation and continue making progress. This could be done through regular check-ins with yourself or by working with a coach or mentor who can provide guidance and support.

Setting realistic expectations is a vital part of building confidence and overcoming self-doubt. By understanding your current abilities, breaking down larger goals into manageable tasks, being flexible, celebrating progress, practicing self-compassion, surrounding yourself with supportive people, and regularly reviewing your goals, you can set yourself up for success.

Progress, not perfection, is the goal, and that each small step you take brings you closer to achieving your dreams.

That's so important it's worth saying again, progress not perfection is the goal.

5: *Seeking Support and Feedback*

No one is an island, and this is especially true when it comes to overcoming self-doubt. Seeking support and feedback from trusted individuals is not a sign of weakness; rather, it is a powerful strategy for building confidence and resilience. In this section, we'll explore the importance of reaching out for support, the benefits of constructive feedback, and how to build a strong network of allies in your journey towards self-assurance.

When you're grappling with self-doubt, it can be incredibly isolating. You might feel like no one else understands your struggles or that asking for help is admitting defeat. However, seeking support is one of the most effective ways to combat these feelings. Surrounding yourself with a network of supportive individuals provides emotional encouragement, practical advice, and a sense of belonging.

Support comes in many forms. It could be a close friend who listens without judgment, a mentor who offers guidance based on their own experiences, or a professional therapist who provides structured help. Each type of support plays a crucial role in helping you navigate your challenges and maintain perspective.

Building a Support Network

Creating a strong support network involves identifying and reaching out to people who can offer different types of assistance. Here are some key individuals to consider including in your network:

Friends and Family: These are the people who know you best and can provide emotional support. They can offer a listening ear, words of encouragement, and a sense of connection.

Mentors: A mentor can provide valuable insights and guidance based on their own experiences. They can help you navigate professional challenges, set realistic goals, and offer constructive feedback.

Peers: Connecting with others who are going through similar experiences can be incredibly validating. Peer support groups, both in-person and online, offer a space to share struggles and successes.

Professionals: Therapists, coaches, and counsellors are trained to help you address self-doubt and build confidence. They can provide strategies and tools tailored to your specific needs.

The Power of Constructive Feedback

Constructive feedback is an essential component of growth. It helps you understand your strengths and areas for improvement from an outside perspective. When you receive feedback, it's important to view it as a tool for growth rather than a personal critique.

Seeking feedback can be daunting, especially if you're already dealing with self-doubt. However, constructive feedback can provide clarity and direction, helping you to see your progress and identify areas for further development. Here's how to make the most of feedback:

Be Open-Minded: Approach feedback with an open mind and a willingness to learn. Remember that the goal is to help you grow, not to tear you down.

Ask for Specifics: When seeking feedback, ask for specific examples and actionable suggestions. This makes the feedback more useful and easier to implement.

Reflect on Feedback: Take time to reflect on the feedback you receive. Consider how it aligns with your own self-assessment and what changes you can make to improve.

Show Gratitude: Thank those who provide feedback. Acknowledging their effort not only fosters positive relationships but also encourages ongoing support.

Overcoming Barriers to Seeking Support

Despite the benefits, many people struggle with seeking support and feedback. Common barriers include fear of judgment, reluctance to burden others, and a belief that one should be able to handle everything alone. Overcoming these barriers involves changing your mindset and recognizing the value of support:

Challenge Negative Beliefs: If you believe that asking for help is a sign of weakness, challenge this thought. Seeking support is a proactive step towards self-improvement and resilience.

Communicate Your Needs: Be clear about what type of support you need. Whether it's a listening ear, advice, or practical assistance, communicating your needs helps others provide the right kind of help.

Start Small: If asking for support feels overwhelming, start with small steps. Share a minor concern with a trusted friend or ask for feedback on a specific task. Gradually, you'll build confidence in seeking support for larger issues.

Seeking support and feedback is a crucial part of overcoming self-doubt and building confidence. By reaching out to trusted individuals, you gain emotional encouragement, practical advice, and valuable insights that help you grow.

You don't have to navigate your challenges alone. Building a strong support network and being open to constructive feedback will empower you to tackle self-doubt and achieve your goals. Embrace the power of community and let others help you on your journey to confidence and self-assurance.

6: Taking Small Steps

Overcoming self-doubt is not an overnight process; it requires taking deliberate and manageable steps towards your goals. By focusing on small, incremental progress, you build momentum and gradually increase your confidence. This approach helps you tackle larger challenges with greater ease and assurance, proving to yourself that you are capable and competent.

One of the most effective strategies to combat self-doubt is to break down your goals into smaller, more achievable tasks. Large goals can often seem overwhelming and unattainable, leading to feelings of inadequacy and hesitation. However, when you divide these goals into smaller steps, they become much more manageable and less intimidating. For instance, if your goal is to write a book, start by outlining a few chapters or writing a certain number of words each day. Each completed task, no matter how small, brings you closer to your ultimate objective and reinforces your belief in your abilities.

Another important aspect of taking small steps is to celebrate each achievement, no matter how minor it may seem. Acknowledging and celebrating your progress provides a sense of accomplishment and motivates you to continue. This positive reinforcement is crucial in building self-confidence and maintaining momentum. For example, if you're working on a fitness goal, celebrate milestones like running a mile without stopping or completing a week of workouts. These celebrations remind you of your capabilities and keep you focused on your progress.

Additionally, taking small steps allows you to adjust and refine your approach as needed. It provides opportunities for learning and growth without the pressure of achieving perfection immediately. This iterative process helps you develop resilience and adaptability, qualities that are essential in overcoming self-doubt. When you encounter setbacks, view them as learning experiences rather than failures. Reflect on what went wrong, make necessary adjustments, and continue moving forward. This mindset shift transforms obstacles into valuable lessons that contribute to your overall growth and success.

Practicing self-compassion is also vital in this journey. Understand that everyone faces challenges and setbacks, and it's okay to not have everything figured out from the start. Treat yourself with the same kindness and understanding you would extend to a friend. When self-doubt creeps in, remind yourself of your past achievements and the progress you've made. This compassionate approach helps mitigate the negative effects of self-doubt and reinforces a positive self-image.

Incorporating mindfulness techniques can further support your efforts in taking small steps. Mindfulness involves being present in the moment and observing your thoughts and feelings without judgment. This practice can help you stay focused on your tasks and reduce anxiety about future outcomes. When you feel overwhelmed by self-doubt, take a moment to breathe deeply and centre yourself. Mindfulness exercises such as meditation, deep breathing, or journaling can help you gain clarity and perspective, making it easier to take purposeful steps towards your goals.

Surrounding yourself with supportive and encouraging individuals can make a significant difference in overcoming self-doubt. Seek out friends, family members, or mentors who believe in your abilities and provide positive reinforcement. Their encouragement can boost your confidence and help you stay motivated. Share your goals and progress with them, and don't hesitate to ask for advice or support when needed. A strong support system provides a safety net that can help you navigate challenges and stay on track.

Taking small, manageable steps is a powerful strategy for overcoming self-doubt and achieving your goals. By breaking down larger objectives into smaller tasks, celebrating your progress, and practicing self-compassion and mindfulness, you build confidence and resilience. Each small step you take is a testament to your capabilities and a significant milestone on your journey towards personal and professional growth. Embrace this approach with patience and determination, and you will gradually overcome self-doubt and unlock your full potential.

7: *Reflecting on Your Journey*

Reflection is a powerful tool that allows us to look back on our experiences, understand our growth, and prepare for future challenges. It is a vital component of personal development, helping us recognize how far we've come and reinforcing the progress we've made. Regular reflection fosters a positive outlook, strengthens motivation, and builds confidence.

When you take the time to reflect on your journey, you acknowledge the efforts and accomplishments that have brought you to where you are today. This practice not only highlights your successes but also sheds light on the lessons learned from setbacks and challenges. Reflection transforms these experiences into valuable insights that guide your future actions and decisions.

Journaling is one of the most effective methods for reflecting on your journey. By writing about your experiences, thoughts, and feelings, you create a tangible record of your progress. Journaling allows you to explore your emotions, identify patterns in your behaviour, and gain a deeper understanding of your motivations and challenges. It provides a safe space to express yourself without judgment and encourages self-discovery and growth.

Start by setting aside a few minutes each day or week to journal. You don't need to write extensively; even a few sentences can be powerful. Focus on key moments, achievements, and challenges you've faced. Consider questions like: What did I learn today? How did I handle a particular situation? What am I proud of? What could I improve? These prompts help you reflect on your journey constructively and with purpose.

Self-assessment is another valuable tool for reflection. Regularly evaluate your progress towards your goals and assess your strengths and areas for improvement. Self-assessment can be done through various methods, such as tracking your achievements, reviewing feedback from others, or using self-assessment questionnaires. This practice helps you stay aware of your growth and ensures you remain aligned with your goals.

To maintain a positive outlook, it's essential to celebrate your achievements, no matter how small they may seem. Recognizing and acknowledging your successes boosts your confidence and motivates you to keep moving forward. Create a habit of celebrating your milestones, whether through a small treat, sharing your success with a friend, or simply taking a moment to appreciate your hard work.

Reflecting on your journey also involves understanding and reframing setbacks. Challenges and failures are inevitable, but they don't define your progress. Instead, view them as opportunities for learning and growth. Ask yourself what you can learn from these experiences and how they can help you improve. By adopting this mindset, you turn obstacles into stepping stones towards your goals.

Visualization is another powerful technique to enhance reflection. Spend time visualizing your journey and envisioning your future achievements. Picture yourself overcoming challenges, reaching your goals, and experiencing the fulfilment of your efforts. Visualization strengthens your commitment to your goals and reinforces your belief in your capabilities.

Incorporating gratitude into your reflection practice can further enhance your positive outlook. Gratitude shifts your focus from what you lack to what you have, fostering a sense of contentment and appreciation. Take a moment each day to list a few things you're grateful for, whether they are related to your progress or other aspects of your life. Gratitude helps you stay grounded and reminds you of the positives in your journey.

Seeking feedback from trusted friends, mentors, or professionals can also enrich your reflection process. External perspectives provide valuable insights and help you see your journey from different angles. Constructive feedback highlights your strengths, identifies areas for improvement, and offers guidance for your next steps. Engage in open and honest conversations with those who support your growth and be receptive to their input.

As you reflect on your journey, it's crucial to practice self-compassion. Treat yourself with the same kindness and understanding you would offer a friend. Acknowledge that growth is a continuous process and that it's okay to have setbacks. Be patient with yourself and recognize that each step, no matter how small, contributes to your overall progress.

Reflecting on your journey is a powerful practice that reinforces your progress, builds confidence, and maintains motivation. By journaling, self-assessing, celebrating achievements, reframing setbacks, visualizing success, practicing gratitude, seeking feedback, and cultivating self-compassion, you create a holistic approach to personal growth.

Embrace reflection as a regular part of your routine, and let it guide you towards continued success and fulfilment on your journey.

Chapter 6: Staying Motivated

"It's time to explore how to stay motivated throughout your journey. We'll guide you on the importance of finding your "why," setting up a reward system, and maintaining a positive attitude.

We'll also cover tips on staying motivated during setbacks and challenges. Let's work together to keep your motivation strong and persistent."

Synopsis

Staying motivated will explore how to maintain your motivation as you pursue your goals and dreams. Staying motivated can be challenging, especially when faced with obstacles and setbacks. With empathy and understanding, I'll share practical strategies to help you stay focused, energized, and inspired throughout your journey.

Finding Your "Why?"

Understanding your core motivations is crucial for sustained effort. We'll delve into the importance of finding your "why" – the deeper reasons behind your goals. By connecting your actions to your values and passions, you'll create a strong foundation for lasting motivation.

Creating a Vision Board

Visualization can be a powerful motivator. We'll guide you through creating a vision board that represents your goals and dreams. By having a visual reminder of what you're working towards, you'll stay inspired and focused on your path.

Developing a Reward System

Rewards can boost motivation by providing positive reinforcement. We'll explore how to set up a reward system that celebrates your progress. This section will include tips on choosing meaningful rewards that encourage you to keep moving forward.

Maintaining a Positive Attitude

A positive attitude can significantly impact your motivation. We'll discuss strategies for cultivating optimism and resilience, such as practicing gratitude, using positive affirmations, and surrounding yourself with uplifting influences.

Overcoming Setbacks and Challenges

Setbacks are inevitable, but they don't have to derail your progress. We'll provide practical advice on how to stay motivated during challenging times. This section will include tips on reframing setbacks as learning opportunities and maintaining your momentum despite obstacles.

Building a Support Network

A strong support network can make a huge difference in staying motivated. We'll talk about the importance of surrounding yourself with positive, encouraging people. This section will offer guidance on how to build and maintain a support network that keeps you accountable and inspired.

Tracking Your Progress

Monitoring your progress can provide a sense of accomplishment and keep you motivated. We'll discuss methods for tracking your achievements, such as journaling, progress charts, and regular self-assessments. Celebrating your milestones will reinforce your commitment and drive.

Adapting to Change

Flexibility is key to staying motivated in the face of change. We'll explore how to adapt your plans and goals as needed, maintaining your motivation even when circumstances shift. This section will emphasize the importance of resilience and adaptability in your journey.

Staying Motivated provides a comprehensive toolkit, remember, motivation is not a constant state but something you cultivate and nurture. With these strategies, you can keep your motivation strong, overcome challenges, and continue making progress towards your goals. Let's stay inspired and energized as we move forward on this journey together.

1: Finding Your "Why?"

Understanding your core motivations is crucial for sustained effort. We'll delve into the importance of finding your "why" – the deeper reasons behind your goals. By connecting your actions to your values and passions, you'll create a strong foundation for lasting motivation.

The Power of Purpose

When you have a clear sense of purpose, every task, no matter how small, feels meaningful. Finding your "why" means understanding the deeper motivations behind your actions. It's about recognizing what truly drives you and aligning your goals with your core values and passions. This deep connection to your purpose can be the difference between fleeting interest and sustained effort.

Living with purpose infuses your actions with a sense of direction and meaning. It provides a compelling reason to wake up each morning and pursue your goals with enthusiasm. A strong "why" can help you navigate the inevitable challenges and setbacks that come with any significant endeavour. It transforms obstacles into opportunities for growth and learning.

Reflecting on Your Values

Start by reflecting on your values. What principles guide your decisions and actions? Are there particular causes or issues that ignite a passion within you? Your values are the bedrock of your motivations. For example, if you value helping others, your "why" might involve making a positive impact on people's lives. Understanding this connection helps you stay committed, even when challenges arise.

Consider creating a list of your core values. These might include things like integrity, compassion, creativity, or adventure. Reflect on how these values have influenced your choices and behaviours in the past. Think about moments when you felt truly fulfilled and aligned with your values. These reflections can provide valuable insights into what motivates you at a deeper level.

Identifying Your Passions

Next, consider your passions. What activities make you lose track of time? What subjects do you love to learn about or discuss? Passion fuels enthusiasm and energy. When your goals align with your passions, they feel less like obligations and more like opportunities for joy and fulfilment. Take some time to explore different interests and see where your passions lie.

Identifying your passions may require some experimentation. Try new activities, explore different hobbies, and pay attention to what excites and energizes you. Passion is often found in activities that challenge you and push you to grow. It's in these moments of flow, where you are fully immersed and engaged, that you can discover what truly lights you up.

Connecting Goals to Your "Why"

Once you've identified your values and passions, connect them to your goals. Ask yourself why each goal is important to you. How does it reflect your values? How does it allow you to engage in your passions? For example, if you aim to start a business, think about why this goal matters. Is it because you want to innovate in your field (passion) and create jobs (value of helping others)? This connection transforms your goals into personal missions.

Consider writing a mission statement for each of your goals. This statement should capture the essence of why the goal matters to you and how it aligns with your values and passions. Refer to these mission statements regularly to remind yourself of your deeper motivations. This practice can provide clarity and focus, especially during challenging times.

Practical Tips to Find Your "Why"

Journaling

Spend time each day reflecting on what matters most to you. Write about your experiences, values, and passions. Journaling can help you uncover patterns and insights that reveal your deeper motivations. Regularly reviewing your journal entries can also provide a sense of continuity and progress in your journey of self-discovery.

Mind Mapping

Create a mind map of your interests and values. Look for patterns and connections that reveal your deeper motivations. Mind mapping is a visual tool that can help you see the relationships between different aspects of your life. It can also stimulate creative thinking and uncover new possibilities for aligning your goals with your "why."

Visioning Exercises

Close your eyes and envision your ideal life. What activities fill your days? What impact are you making? This vision can help clarify your "why." Spend time regularly engaging in visioning exercises to keep your goals and motivations vivid and inspiring. Visualization can also help you overcome obstacles by keeping your focus on the positive outcomes you are working towards.

Sustaining Motivation

Your "why" is a powerful motivator. When you encounter obstacles, reminding yourself of your core reasons can reignite your drive. Keep visual and written reminders of your "why" in places you'll see them regularly. This constant reinforcement helps maintain focus and resilience, turning temporary setbacks into stepping stones towards your ultimate goals.

Consider creating a personal mantra or affirmation that encapsulates your "why." Repeat this mantra to yourself daily, especially during challenging moments. Sharing your "why" with supportive friends and family members can also provide additional encouragement and accountability. By keeping your motivations front and centre, you can sustain your effort and achieve your goals with confidence and clarity.

Finding your "why" is a journey of self-discovery that requires reflection, exploration, and connection. By understanding your core motivations, you can align your actions with your values and passions, creating a strong foundation for lasting motivation and fulfilment.

Embrace this journey with curiosity and openness and let your "why" guide you towards a life of purpose and meaning.

2: Creating a Vision Board

Visualization can be a powerful motivator. We'll guide you through creating a vision board that represents your goals and dreams. By having a visual reminder of what you're working towards, you'll stay inspired and focused on your path.

Visualization is a technique where you create a mental image of a desired outcome. This practice can significantly enhance motivation and focus. A vision board takes this concept further by providing a tangible, visual representation of your goals. It serves as a daily reminder of what you're working towards, keeping your aspirations front and centre.

When you visualize your goals, you're not just daydreaming; you're actively programming your mind to pursue those aspirations. Visualization helps to bridge the gap between where you are and where you want to be. It turns abstract ideas into concrete images, making your dreams feel more attainable. This technique can boost your confidence, enhance your focus, and increase your overall motivation.

Getting Started with Your Vision Board

Creating a vision board is an enjoyable and inspiring process. Begin by gathering materials such as magazines, photos, scissors, glue, and a large piece of poster board or corkboard. The goal is to fill your board with images and words that represent your dreams and aspirations.

Think about the different areas of your life that you want to focus on, such as career, relationships, health, personal growth, and hobbies. Each of these areas can be represented on your vision board. This holistic approach ensures that you're visualizing a well-rounded and fulfilling life.

Selecting Images and Words

Choose images that resonate with your goals. These could be photos, magazine clippings, or printed images from the internet. Look for pictures that evoke strong positive emotions and align with your "why." For instance, if one of your goals is to travel more, include pictures of destinations you dream of visiting.

In addition to images, include words and phrases that inspire you. These could be affirmations, quotes, or single words that capture the essence of your goals. Words like "success," "adventure," or "creativity" can reinforce your aspirations and keep you motivated. The right words can act as powerful triggers, reminding you of your purpose and pushing you forward when you face challenges.

Assembling Your Vision Board

Start arranging your images and words on the board. There's no right or wrong way to do this—let your creativity guide you. Some people prefer a neat and orderly layout, while others opt for a more freeform, collage-like style. The key is to create a board that feels inspiring and energizing to you.

Once you're satisfied with the arrangement, start gluing or pinning the items to the board. As you work, take time to reflect on each image and word. Think about why it's important to you and how it represents your goals. This mindfulness enhances the visualization process, making your vision board a powerful tool for motivation.

Displaying Your Vision Board

Place your vision board in a location where you'll see it daily. This could be in your office, bedroom, or any space you spend a lot of time in. The constant visual reminder keeps your goals at the forefront of your mind, reinforcing your commitment and motivation.

By regularly viewing your vision board, you maintain a clear focus on your aspirations and stay aligned with your "why."

As your goals evolve, so should your vision board. Update it with new images and words that reflect your current aspirations. Life is dynamic, and your vision board should be too. Periodically review and refresh your board to ensure it remains relevant and inspiring.

Use Affirmations

Include positive affirmations that boost your confidence and reinforce your goals. Affirmations are powerful statements that can reprogram your subconscious mind. Phrases like "I am capable," "I am deserving of success," and "I attract positive opportunities" can help you maintain a positive mindset and overcome self-doubt.

Engage Your Senses

Consider adding tactile elements like fabric swatches or small objects that represent your goals. Engaging multiple senses can make your vision board more impactful.

The tactile experience can deepen your connection to your goals and make the visualization process more immersive.

Your vision board should reflect your unique aspirations and style. Don't worry about making it perfect; focus on making it meaningful to you. The more personal and authentic your vision board is, the more effective it will be in motivating you.

Reflect and Visualize Daily

Spend a few minutes each day reflecting on your vision board. Close your eyes and visualize yourself achieving your goals. Imagine the emotions you'll feel and the sense of accomplishment you'll experience. This daily practice can strengthen your resolve and keep you focused on your path.

Creating a vision board is a powerful step towards manifesting your dreams. By visually representing your goals, you keep your aspirations alive and present in your everyday life. This constant visual reminder helps you stay inspired, focused, and motivated, turning your dreams into reality.

3: Developing a Reward System

Rewards can boost motivation by providing positive reinforcement. We'll explore how to set up a reward system that celebrates your progress. This section will include tips on choosing meaningful rewards that encourage you to keep moving forward.

Rewards are powerful motivators that can reinforce positive behaviours and achievements. By acknowledging and celebrating your progress, you create a cycle of positive reinforcement that encourages continued effort and commitment. A well-structured reward system can help you stay motivated, even when the journey towards your goals becomes challenging.

Understanding What Motivates You

The first step in developing a reward system is understanding what motivates you. Different people are driven by different types of rewards. For some, tangible rewards like a new book or a special treat can be highly motivating. For others, intangible rewards such as personal satisfaction, recognition, or time spent on a favourite hobby can be equally effective. It's important to tailor your reward system to what genuinely excites and motivates you.

Spend some time reflecting on what types of rewards have motivated you in the past. Think about both tangible and intangible rewards. For instance, you might have found that treating yourself to a new gadget after completing a project was very motivating. Alternatively, you might have felt deeply satisfied and motivated by personal recognition or the sense of achievement from mastering a new skill.

Consider creating a list of potential rewards that you find motivating. This list can serve as a starting point for setting up your reward system. Remember, the most effective rewards are those that you look forward to and that feel truly rewarding.

Setting Milestones and Rewards

Break down your larger goals into smaller, manageable milestones. Each milestone represents a step towards your ultimate objective and provides an opportunity to celebrate progress. For example, if your goal is to run a marathon, set milestones for completing your first 5K, 10K, and half marathon. Assign a reward for each milestone, ensuring it's something you genuinely look forward to.

Setting milestones helps to make large goals feel more attainable. Each milestone achieved is a step closer to your goal and provides a natural point for celebration. This approach helps to maintain momentum and keeps you engaged with your goal over the long term.

Creating a Milestone Plan

Develop a plan that outlines your milestones and the corresponding rewards. For each milestone, specify what needs to be accomplished and the reward you'll give yourself upon completion. This plan serves as a roadmap and provides clear markers for progress. Having a written plan also helps to keep you accountable and focused.

Choosing Meaningful Rewards

The key to an effective reward system is choosing rewards that are meaningful and motivating to you. Here are some ideas for different types of rewards:

- **Tangible Rewards:** These can include items like books, gadgets, or clothing. Choose something you've been wanting but have held off on purchasing.
- **Experiential Rewards:** Plan a special outing or activity, such as a spa day, a weekend getaway, or tickets to a concert or event.
- **Personal Rewards:** Allow yourself extra time for a favourite hobby, a relaxing bath, or a movie night. These rewards offer personal satisfaction and relaxation.

When selecting rewards, consider their significance and how they align with your values and passions. The more meaningful the reward, the more motivated you'll be to earn it.

Once you've set your milestones and chosen your rewards, it's time to implement your system. Keep track of your progress and celebrate each milestone as you reach it. Maintaining a visual chart or journal can help you see how far you've come and keep you motivated to continue.

Tracking Progress

Use a method that works best for you to track your progress. This could be a journal, a spreadsheet, or a visual chart. Regularly update your tracking system to reflect your achievements. Seeing your progress in a tangible format can be incredibly motivating and reinforces the positive behaviours that help you reach your goals.

Celebrating Milestones

When you reach a milestone, take the time to celebrate. Savor the moment and enjoy your reward. Reflect on the effort and dedication that brought you to this point. Celebrating milestones is not just about the reward; it's also about recognizing your hard work and commitment.

Be Consistent

Ensure you follow through with your rewards. Consistency reinforces the positive behaviour and keeps you motivated. If you set a reward, make sure you give it to yourself when you achieve the corresponding milestone. This consistency helps to build trust in your reward system and ensures that it remains an effective motivator.

Mix It Up

Vary your rewards to keep things interesting. Avoid becoming too predictable or repetitive, as this can diminish the motivational impact. Incorporate a mix of tangible and intangible rewards and consider switching them up periodically to maintain excitement and interest.

Balance Immediate and Long-Term Rewards

Include both immediate rewards for short-term milestones and larger rewards for long-term goals. This balance keeps you motivated throughout the journey. Immediate rewards provide quick reinforcement, while long-term rewards give you something significant to strive for.

By recognizing and celebrating your progress, you reinforce positive behaviours and build momentum towards achieving your goals. An effective reward system not only boosts motivation but also makes the journey more enjoyable and fulfilling. Embrace the process of rewarding yourself and let it drive you towards your aspirations with enthusiasm and determination.

4: Maintaining a Positive Attitude

Maintaining a positive attitude is a cornerstone of motivation and personal success. A positive mindset not only enhances your mental and emotional well-being but also empowers you to face challenges with resilience and determination. Let's explore some effective strategies for cultivating and maintaining optimism and resilience in your daily life.

One of the most powerful tools for maintaining a positive attitude is the practice of gratitude. Gratitude involves recognizing and appreciating the good things in your life, no matter how small. This practice can shift your focus from what you lack to what you have, fostering a sense of abundance and contentment. To incorporate gratitude into your daily routine, consider keeping a gratitude journal. Each day, write down three things you are grateful for. These can range from major life events to simple pleasures like a beautiful sunset or a kind word from a friend. Over time, this practice can rewire your brain to notice and appreciate the positive aspects of your life, boosting your overall happiness and well-being.

Positive affirmations are another effective strategy for maintaining a positive attitude. Affirmations are positive statements that you repeat to yourself to challenge and overcome negative thoughts. They can help you build confidence and resilience by reinforcing a positive self-image. For example, you might say to yourself, "I am capable and strong," or "I am worthy of success and happiness." The key to effective affirmations is consistency. Repeat your affirmations daily, preferably in front of a mirror, and believe in the words you are saying. Over time, these positive messages can become ingrained in your subconscious mind, helping you to stay motivated and focused on your goals.

Surrounding yourself with uplifting influences is also crucial for maintaining a positive attitude. The people you spend time with can significantly impact your mood and outlook on life. Seek out individuals who inspire and support you and limit your exposure to those who bring negativity or drain your energy. Positive relationships can provide emotional support, encouragement, and a sense of belonging, all of which are essential for maintaining a positive mindset.

In addition to cultivating a supportive social network, consider the impact of your environment on your attitude. Create a space that reflects positivity and inspiration. This could involve decorating your home or workspace with uplifting quotes, photos of loved ones, or items that bring you joy. A positive environment can serve as a constant reminder of your goals and the positive aspects of your life, helping you to stay focused and motivated.

Mindfulness and meditation are powerful practices for maintaining a positive attitude. Mindfulness involves being fully present in the moment and observing your thoughts and feelings without judgment. This practice can help you become more aware of negative thought patterns and develop a more compassionate and accepting attitude towards yourself. Meditation, on the other hand, involves focusing your mind on a particular object, thought, or activity to achieve a state of calm and relaxation. Both practices can reduce stress, improve emotional regulation, and enhance overall well-being. To get started with mindfulness and meditation, consider setting aside a few minutes each day to sit quietly and focus on your breath. Gradually increase the duration of your practice as you become more comfortable with the techniques.

Another effective strategy for maintaining a positive attitude is to set realistic and achievable goals. Having clear, attainable goals gives you a sense of purpose and direction, which can boost your motivation and self-esteem. Break down your larger goals into smaller, manageable tasks, and celebrate your progress along the way. This approach not only makes your goals feel more attainable but also provides regular opportunities for positive reinforcement and a sense of accomplishment.

Physical activity is another powerful tool for maintaining a positive attitude. Exercise releases endorphins, which are natural mood enhancers. Regular physical activity can reduce stress, anxiety, and depression, while also improving your overall physical health. Find an activity that you enjoy, whether it's walking, dancing, swimming, or yoga, and incorporate it into your daily routine. Even a short burst of physical activity can have a significant impact on your mood and energy levels.

It's also important to practice self-compassion. Treat yourself with the same kindness and understanding that you would offer to a friend. Acknowledge your efforts and progress and be gentle with yourself when you encounter setbacks. Self-compassion involves recognizing that everyone makes mistakes and that it's okay to be imperfect. By practicing self-compassion, you can build resilience and maintain a positive attitude even in the face of challenges.

Laughter is a natural antidote to stress and negativity. Find ways to incorporate humour and playfulness into your daily life. Watch a funny movie, read a humorous book, or spend time with people who make you laugh. Laughter can boost your mood, strengthen your immune system, and provide a sense of connection with others.

Remember that maintaining a positive attitude is a continuous process. It's normal to have days when you feel less positive or motivated. The key is to be persistent and consistent in your efforts to cultivate optimism and resilience. Regularly check in with yourself and assess your mental and emotional state. If you notice negative thoughts creeping in, take proactive steps to shift your mindset. This could involve practicing gratitude, repeating positive affirmations, or engaging in a physical activity that you enjoy.

Maintaining a positive attitude is essential for personal growth and motivation. By practicing gratitude, using positive affirmations, surrounding yourself with uplifting influences, and incorporating mindfulness, physical activity, and self-compassion into your daily routine, you can cultivate a resilient and optimistic mindset.

It's okay to have setbacks and that the journey towards a positive attitude is an ongoing process. Embrace the strategies that work best for you and stay committed to fostering a positive outlook on life. With a positive attitude, you can overcome challenges, achieve your goals, and lead a more fulfilling and joyful life.

5: Overcoming Setbacks and Challenges

Setbacks are an inevitable part of any journey toward achieving your goals. While they can be discouraging and frustrating, they don't have to derail your progress. In fact, setbacks can offer valuable learning opportunities and can help you build resilience and strength. In this section, we will provide practical advice on how to stay motivated during challenging times, how to reframe setbacks as learning opportunities, and how to maintain your momentum despite obstacles.

Embracing Setbacks as Part of the Journey

The first step in overcoming setbacks is to embrace them as a natural part of the journey. Everyone encounters obstacles, and experiencing setbacks does not mean you are failing. Rather, it is a sign that you are pushing your boundaries and striving for growth. By accepting that setbacks are inevitable, you can approach them with a more positive and resilient mindset.

When you face a setback, take a moment to acknowledge your feelings. It's natural to feel disappointed or frustrated but try not to dwell on these emotions for too long. Instead, shift your focus to what you can learn from the experience and how you can move forward.

One of the most powerful ways to overcome setbacks is to reframe them as learning opportunities. Each setback provides a chance to gain new insights, develop new skills, and grow stronger. By viewing setbacks through this lens, you can turn challenges into stepping stones toward your ultimate goals.

Analysing the Setback

When you encounter a setback, take some time to analyse what happened. Ask yourself the following questions:

- What specific factors contributed to the setback?
- Were there any warning signs or red flags that you missed?
- What could you have done differently to prevent or mitigate the setback?

Reflecting on these questions can help you identify the root causes of the setback and develop strategies to avoid similar issues in the future.

Next, focus on extracting lessons from the setback. Consider what you have learned from the experience and how you can apply these lessons moving forward. For example, if you missed a deadline because you underestimated the amount of time a task would take, you might learn to build in buffer time for future projects. By turning setbacks into valuable lessons, you can continuously improve and grow.

Maintaining momentum during challenging times can be difficult, but it is crucial for staying on track toward your goals. Here are some strategies to help you stay motivated and keep moving forward, even when faced with obstacles.

Setting Short-Term Goals

When you encounter a setback, it can be helpful to set short-term goals that are more easily attainable. These smaller goals can provide a sense of accomplishment and help you regain your confidence and motivation. Break down your larger goals into smaller, manageable tasks, and focus on achieving these incremental milestones. Each small victory can boost your morale and keep you moving in the right direction.

Focusing on What You Can Control

During challenging times, it's important to focus on what you can control rather than what you can't. There are always factors outside of your control that can impact your progress, but dwelling on these factors can lead to feelings of helplessness and frustration. Instead, direct your energy toward the aspects of the situation that you can influence. By taking proactive steps to address the areas within your control, you can regain a sense of agency and momentum.

Practicing Self-Compassion

Self-compassion is essential for maintaining motivation during setbacks. Treat yourself with the same kindness and understanding that you would offer to a friend who is facing a challenge. Acknowledge your efforts and progress and be gentle with yourself when things don't go as planned. Remember that setbacks are a normal part of the journey, and they do not define your worth or capabilities.

Don't be afraid to seek support from others when you encounter setbacks. Reach out to friends, family members, or mentors who can offer encouragement, advice, and a fresh perspective. Sometimes, talking through a challenge with someone you trust can help you see the situation more clearly and identify potential solutions. Additionally, joining a support group or finding an accountability partner can provide ongoing motivation and camaraderie.

Maintaining a positive attitude is crucial for overcoming setbacks. While it's natural to feel discouraged at times, try to focus on the progress you have made and the possibilities that lie ahead. Surround yourself with positive influences, such as inspiring books, podcasts, or motivational quotes. By cultivating a positive mindset, you can build resilience and stay motivated, even in the face of challenges.

Visualizing Success

Visualization is a powerful tool for maintaining motivation and overcoming setbacks. Spend time each day visualizing yourself achieving your goals and overcoming obstacles. Imagine how it will feel to reach your desired outcome and the sense of accomplishment you will experience. Visualization can help you stay focused on your goals and reinforce your belief in your ability to succeed.

Developing a Resilient Mindset

Building resilience is key to overcoming setbacks and maintaining long-term motivation. Resilience is the ability to bounce back from challenges and keep moving forward, even when the going gets tough. Here are some strategies for developing a resilient mindset:

Change is a constant part of life, and being able to adapt to change is a crucial aspect of resilience. Embrace change as an opportunity for growth and learning. Rather than resisting change, try to see it as a chance to develop new skills and perspectives.

A growth mindset is the belief that your abilities and intelligence can be developed through effort and learning. By adopting a growth mindset, you can view setbacks as opportunities for growth rather than as failures. Embrace challenges, persist in the face of obstacles, and learn from criticism. This mindset can help you stay motivated and resilient, even when you encounter setbacks.

Patience is an important aspect of resilience. Understand that achieving your goals takes time and that setbacks are a natural part of the process. Cultivate patience by focusing on the journey rather than the destination. Celebrate your progress, no matter how small, and trust that your efforts will pay off in the long run.

Mindfulness involves being fully present in the moment and observing your thoughts and feelings without judgment. Practicing mindfulness can help you stay grounded and focused, even during challenging times. It can also reduce stress and improve your emotional regulation. Consider incorporating mindfulness practices, such as meditation or deep breathing exercises, into your daily routine to build resilience and maintain a positive attitude.

Overcoming setbacks and challenges is an essential part of achieving your goals and personal growth. By embracing setbacks as part of the journey, reframing them as learning opportunities, and maintaining momentum despite obstacles, you can stay motivated and resilient. Cultivating a positive attitude, practicing self-compassion, seeking support, and developing a resilient mindset are all key strategies for navigating setbacks and continuing your path to success. Remember, setbacks do not define you; it is how you respond to them that matters most. Embrace the journey, learn from your experiences, and stay committed to your goals. With resilience and determination, you can overcome any challenge and achieve your aspirations.

6: Tracking Your Progress

Tracking your progress is a fundamental aspect of achieving your goals. It not only provides a sense of accomplishment but also keeps you motivated and focused. By monitoring your achievements, you can celebrate your milestones, reinforce your commitment, and drive towards your objectives with renewed enthusiasm. In this section, we will explore various methods for tracking your progress, including journaling, progress charts, and regular self-assessments.

Tracking your progress allows you to see how far you've come and what you have accomplished. It provides tangible evidence of your efforts and helps you stay motivated, especially when you encounter challenges. By regularly monitoring your progress, you can identify patterns, adjust, and ensure that you are on the right path toward your goals.

Journaling

Journaling is a powerful tool for tracking your progress. It provides a space for you to reflect on your experiences, record your achievements, and process your thoughts and emotions. A journal can serve as a personal record of your journey, offering insights into your growth and development over time.

To begin journaling, choose a format that works best for you. This could be a traditional notebook, a digital journal, or a combination of both. The key is to find a method that you feel comfortable with and that you will use consistently.

What to Include in Your Journal

When journaling, consider including the following elements:

Daily Reflections: Write about your experiences, thoughts, and feelings each day. Reflect on what you accomplished, what challenges you faced, and how you overcame them.

Goal Tracking: Record your goals and the steps you are taking to achieve them. Note any milestones you reach and celebrate your progress.

Lessons Learned: Reflect on any insights or lessons you gained from your experiences. This can help you grow and improve as you move forward.

Gratitude: Include a section for gratitude, where you write about the things you are grateful for. This can help you maintain a positive mindset and stay motivated.

Journaling offers numerous benefits, including:

Clarity: Writing about your goals and progress can help you clarify your thoughts and gain a better understanding of your journey.

Accountability: Keeping a journal holds you accountable to yourself. It provides a record of your commitments and helps you stay on track.

Reflection: Journaling allows you to reflect on your experiences and learn from them. It can provide valuable insights into your strengths and areas for improvement.

Progress Charts

Progress charts are visual tools that can help you track your achievements and stay motivated. They provide a clear and tangible representation of your progress, making it easier to see how far you've come and what you still need to accomplish.

To create a progress chart, start by defining your goals and the milestones you want to track. Use a chart format that works best for you, such as a bar chart, line graph, or checklist. You can create your chart on paper, use a digital tool, or find an app that offers progress tracking features.

Update your progress chart regularly to reflect your achievements. This could be done daily, weekly, or monthly, depending on your goals and preferences. Seeing your progress visually can provide a sense of accomplishment and motivate you to keep moving forward.

Progress charts offer several advantages:

Motivation: Seeing your progress visually can boost your motivation and encourage you to continue working towards your goals.

Accountability: A progress chart holds you accountable and provides a clear record of your achievements.

Focus: Tracking your progress helps you stay focused on your goals and the steps you need to take to achieve them.

Regular Self-Assessments

Regular self-assessments are essential for tracking your progress and making adjustments as needed. By evaluating your performance and reflecting on your achievements, you can identify areas for improvement and ensure that you are on the right path toward your goals.

To conduct a self-assessment, set aside regular intervals to evaluate your progress. This could be done weekly, monthly, or quarterly, depending on your goals and preferences. During your self-assessment, consider the following questions:

What have I accomplished since my last assessment?

What challenges did I face, and how did I overcome them?

What lessons have I learned?

What adjustments do I need to make to stay on track?

Self-assessments offer several benefits:

Insight: Regular self-assessments provide valuable insights into your progress and performance. They help you identify strengths and areas for improvement.

Accountability: Assessing your progress holds you accountable and ensures that you are taking the necessary steps toward your goals.

Adaptability: Self-assessments allow you to make adjustments and adapt your approach as needed. This ensures that you stay on track and continue making progress.

Celebrating Milestones

Celebrating your milestones is an important aspect of tracking your progress. It provides a sense of accomplishment and reinforces your commitment to your goals. By acknowledging and celebrating your achievements, you can maintain your motivation and drive.

When you reach a milestone, take the time to celebrate your achievement. This could be done in various ways, such as:

Treating Yourself: Reward yourself with something special, such as a favourite treat, a new book, or a relaxing day off.

Sharing Your Success: Share your achievement with friends, family, or a support group. Celebrating with others can enhance your sense of accomplishment and provide additional encouragement.

Reflecting on Your Journey: Take a moment to reflect on your journey and the steps you took to reach your milestone. Acknowledge your hard work and the progress you've made.

Celebrating milestones offers several benefits:

Motivation: Celebrating your achievements can boost your motivation and encourage you to continue working toward your goals.

Positive Reinforcement: Recognizing your accomplishments reinforces positive behaviours and helps you stay committed to your goals.

Satisfaction: Celebrating your milestones provides a sense of satisfaction and fulfilment, enhancing your overall well-being.

Tracking your progress is a crucial aspect of achieving your goals and maintaining motivation. By using methods such as journaling, progress charts, and regular self-assessments, you can monitor your achievements, celebrate your milestones, and stay focused on your objectives.

Embrace the journey, acknowledge your progress, and celebrate your successes along the way. By doing so, you will build momentum, reinforce your commitment, and continue to move forward with confidence and determination.

7: *Adapting to Change*

Adapting to change is an essential skill in the journey of personal growth and achieving goals. Flexibility allows us to remain motivated and focused, even when faced with unexpected shifts in our circumstances. This chapter will delve into the importance of resilience and adaptability, providing strategies to help you navigate changes while maintaining your motivation and commitment.

Change is an inevitable part of life. Whether it's a change in your personal life, career, or external environment, adapting to new situations can be challenging. The key to thriving amidst change is to embrace it rather than resist it. When we accept that change is a natural part of our journey, we can approach it with a positive and proactive mindset.

One of the first steps in adapting to change is recognizing that your plans and goals may need to be adjusted. This does not mean abandoning your aspirations, but rather, being open to modifying the path you take to achieve them. Flexibility in your approach allows you to stay aligned with your overall objectives while accommodating new realities.

To adapt effectively, it's crucial to maintain a clear understanding of your core goals and values. These serve as your guiding principles, helping you make informed decisions even when the landscape changes. Regularly revisiting and reaffirming your goals can provide a sense of stability and direction during uncertain times.

When faced with change, it's helpful to break down your larger goals into smaller, manageable tasks. This approach makes it easier to adapt your plans and stay on track. By focusing on one step at a time, you can maintain a sense of progress and control, which is vital for staying motivated.

Another important aspect of adapting to change is developing a growth mindset. This mindset embraces challenges and views them as opportunities for learning and growth. When you encounter setbacks or obstacles, instead of seeing them as failures, consider what you can learn from the experience and how you can use it to improve. This perspective not only builds resilience but also fosters a positive attitude towards change.

Change Happens, So Stay Flexible

Flexibility also involves being open to new ideas and approaches. Sometimes, change can present opportunities that you hadn't considered before. By staying open-minded and willing to explore different possibilities, you can discover new paths to achieving your goals. This adaptability can lead to unexpected and rewarding outcomes.

One practical strategy for adapting to change is to regularly review and update your action plans. Life is dynamic, and your plans should reflect that. Set aside time to assess your progress and make necessary adjustments. This could involve shifting deadlines, reallocating resources, or revising your priorities. By staying proactive and responsive, you can ensure that your plans remain relevant and effective.

It's also important to practice self-care during times of change. Adjusting to new circumstances can be stressful, and taking care of your physical and mental well-being is essential. Ensure that you maintain healthy habits, such as regular exercise, adequate sleep, and a balanced diet. Additionally, practice mindfulness or meditation to help manage stress and maintain a positive outlook.

Support from others can be invaluable when adapting to change. Reach out to friends, family, or mentors for guidance and encouragement. Sharing your experiences and seeking advice can provide new perspectives and help you navigate challenges more effectively. Surrounding yourself with a supportive network can also boost your resilience and motivation.

Resilience is a crucial component of adapting to change. It involves the ability to bounce back from setbacks and continue moving forward. Building resilience takes time and practice, but it's a skill that can be developed. Focus on building your emotional strength by setting realistic expectations, managing stress, and maintaining a positive attitude. Remember that resilience is not about avoiding difficulties but rather about facing them with courage and determination.

Celebrate your adaptability and progress. Acknowledge the efforts you put into adjusting your plans and overcoming challenges. Celebrating small victories along the way reinforces your commitment and motivation. It also reminds you of your capability to handle change and continue striving towards your goals.

Adapting to change is an essential skill for maintaining motivation and achieving long-term success. By embracing flexibility, developing a growth mindset, and practicing resilience, you can navigate changes with confidence and continue making progress towards your goals.

Change is an opportunity for growth and learning. With the right mindset and strategies, you can turn challenges into stepping stones on your journey to personal and professional fulfilment.

Chapter 7: Accountability and Support Systems

"Together we'll explore the power of accountability and support. It will explain how you can leverage accountability partners, mentors, and support groups to stay on track.

Building a strong support system can significantly boost your confidence and productivity. Let's discover how these connections can help you achieve your goals and maintain your motivation."

Synopsis

In Chapter 7, we'll explore the vital role that accountability and support systems play in your journey towards achieving your goals. Having a network of supportive individuals and structures can significantly enhance your motivation, consistency, and overall success. Let's delve into how you can build and utilize these systems effectively.

The Power of Accountability

Accountability is a powerful motivator. In this section, we'll discuss how having someone to hold you accountable can keep you on track. Whether it's a friend, mentor, or coach, knowing that someone is watching your progress can push you to stay committed and take consistent action.

Choosing an Accountability Partner

Not all accountability partners are created equal. We'll explore the qualities to look for in an accountability partner and how to establish a mutually beneficial relationship. This section will provide tips on finding the right person who can support and challenge you effectively.

Using Technology for Accountability and Support

Technology offers various tools to help you stay accountable and connected. We'll introduce apps and platforms that facilitate goal tracking, progress sharing, and virtual support. This section will help you leverage technology to enhance your accountability and support system.

Setting Up Regular Check-Ins

Regular check-ins are essential for maintaining accountability and receiving ongoing support. We'll discuss how to set up effective check-ins with your accountability partner or support network. This section will cover the frequency, structure, and content of these check-ins to ensure they are productive and motivating.

Balancing Independence and Support

While support systems are crucial, it's also important to maintain a sense of independence. We'll explore how to balance seeking support with taking personal responsibility for your goals. This section will help you develop a healthy reliance on your support network while fostering self-motivation and resilience.

This will give you a clear understanding of how to build and utilize accountability and support systems to enhance your journey. Remember, you don't have to go through this alone. Surrounding yourself with the right people and structures can provide the encouragement, motivation, and guidance you need to achieve your goals.

1: The Power of Accountability

Accountability is a significant driving force when it comes to achieving goals and maintaining motivation. The presence of someone to hold you accountable can be the difference between giving up and persevering, especially when challenges arise. Knowing that someone else is aware of your goals and progress can instil a sense of responsibility and commitment that fuels continuous effort and dedication.

Accountability means being answerable for your actions and progress to someone other than yourself. It involves having a partner, mentor, coach, or group to whom you report your progress, discuss your challenges, and celebrate your successes. This external support can provide a fresh perspective, encouragement, and constructive feedback, making the journey towards your goals less solitary and more structured.

Accountability Partners

An accountability partner can take various forms. It could be a friend who shares similar goals, a mentor with more experience in your field, or a coach who specializes in helping people achieve their objectives. The key is to choose someone who is supportive, trustworthy, and willing to challenge you when necessary. The right accountability partner can help you stay focused, motivated, and on track.

When you know that someone is expecting updates on your progress, you are more likely to stay committed to your tasks and goals. This external pressure can help you push through procrastination and maintain a steady pace of progress.

Regular check-ins with an accountability partner can provide ongoing motivation. The encouragement and support you receive can boost your morale and keep you inspired, even when the journey gets tough.

An accountability partner can offer a different viewpoint on your challenges and achievements. This external perspective can help you see things more clearly, identify areas for improvement, and recognize accomplishments you might have overlooked.

Having scheduled check-ins creates a sense of structure and routine. These regular meetings can help you break down your goals into manageable tasks and ensure that you are making consistent progress.

Choosing an Accountability Partner

Selecting the right accountability partner is crucial. Look for someone who:

Shares Similar Goals: A partner who understands your objectives and is also working towards their own goals can create a mutually beneficial relationship.
Is Trustworthy: Trust and confidentiality are essential. You need to feel comfortable sharing your progress, challenges, and setbacks.
Provides Constructive Feedback: An effective accountability partner offers honest and helpful feedback, helping you stay on course without being overly critical.
Is Reliable: Consistency in check-ins and availability is important. Your partner should be committed to the process and regular meetings.

Tips for Effective Accountability

From the outset, establish clear expectations for your accountability relationship. Discuss how often you will check in, the format of your updates, and what kind of support each of you needs. Setting these expectations helps ensure a smooth and productive partnership.

Schedule regular check-ins, whether weekly, bi-weekly, or monthly. Consistency is key to maintaining momentum and ensuring that accountability remains a priority.

During your check-ins, be honest about your progress, challenges, and any obstacles you're facing. Transparency is essential for receiving meaningful support and feedback.

Acknowledge and celebrate your achievements, no matter how small. Celebrating milestones with your accountability partner reinforces positive behaviour and keeps motivation high.

Be flexible and willing to adjust your approach if something isn't working. If you find that your check-ins are becoming less effective, discuss it with your partner and make the necessary changes.

Accountability partnerships can face challenges, such as conflicting schedules or differing expectations. Open communication is vital in addressing these issues. If problems arise, discuss them openly and work together to find solutions that keep both partners engaged and motivated.

Building a Supportive Network

Beyond individual accountability partnerships, consider joining or forming a support group with like-minded individuals. Group accountability can provide a broader network of support and a sense of community. Sharing experiences, challenges, and successes with a group can enhance your motivation and provide diverse perspectives.

Accountability is a powerful tool for achieving goals and maintaining motivation. By having someone to hold you accountable, you gain a sense of responsibility, increased commitment, and ongoing support. Whether through an individual partner or a supportive group, accountability can help you stay focused, overcome challenges, and achieve your objectives. Remember, the journey is more enjoyable and successful when shared with others who are committed to your growth and success.

2: Choosing an Accountability Partner

Finding the right accountability partner can be a transformative experience in your journey towards achieving your goals. Not all accountability partners are created equal, and the success of this partnership largely depends on choosing the right person who can support, motivate, and challenge you effectively. Let's explore the qualities to look for in an accountability partner and how to establish a mutually beneficial relationship.

The first step in selecting an accountability partner is to identify someone who shares your commitment to personal growth and development. This doesn't necessarily mean that they need to have the same goals as you, but they should have a similar level of dedication and enthusiasm for self-improvement. When both partners are equally invested in the process, it creates a balanced and supportive dynamic where each person feels motivated to stay on track.

One of the most important qualities to look for in an accountability partner is reliability. This person should be dependable and consistent in their communication and follow-through. Reliability builds trust, which is the foundation of any successful partnership. If you know that your partner will check in with you regularly and hold you accountable for your commitments, it significantly increases your chances of staying motivated and achieving your goals.

Another essential quality is honesty. Your accountability partner should be able to provide constructive feedback in a supportive manner. They should be able to point out areas where you might be falling short or where you could improve, but also celebrate your successes and progress. Honest feedback helps you gain a clearer perspective on your efforts and encourages continuous improvement. It's important that this honesty is paired with empathy, so the feedback is received as supportive rather than critical.

Compatibility in terms of communication style is also crucial. Some people prefer frequent, detailed check-ins, while others might find this overwhelming and prefer more occasional, high-level updates. It's important to discuss and agree on the frequency and format of your check-ins early on to ensure that both partners are comfortable with the arrangement. Clear communication helps to avoid misunderstandings and ensures that both parties are on the same page.

Finding the right accountability partner also involves setting clear expectations and boundaries. From the outset, discuss what each of you hopes to gain from the partnership and how you plan to support each other. Establishing ground rules about how often you'll check in, the types of feedback you'll provide, and the confidentiality of your discussions can prevent potential issues and ensure a smooth partnership. Remember, this relationship should be mutually beneficial, so it's important to balance your needs with those of your partner.

Choose Someone with a Different Viewpoint

It's also helpful to choose someone who can offer a different perspective or expertise. If your accountability partner has knowledge or experience in areas where you're seeking to improve, they can provide valuable insights and advice. This diversity in perspectives can enrich your journey and provide new strategies for overcoming challenges.

When selecting an accountability partner, consider their availability and willingness to commit time to the partnership. It's important that they have the capacity to engage regularly and meaningfully in your check-ins. If either partner feels that they're unable to dedicate sufficient time, it could lead to frustration and a lack of progress. Be upfront about your availability and ensure that your partner can match that commitment.

Building a strong accountability partnership also involves being open to receiving and giving feedback. Constructive feedback should be seen as a tool for growth rather than criticism. When receiving feedback, try to remain open-minded and consider it as an opportunity to learn and improve. Similarly, when providing feedback, focus on being supportive and offering actionable suggestions rather than simply pointing out shortcomings.

One effective strategy for finding an accountability partner is to look within your existing network. Friends, family members, colleagues, or members of a community group your part of can be great candidates. These individuals already know you and your personality, which can make the partnership more comfortable and effective from the start. However, it's important to choose someone who can maintain a professional and supportive relationship without allowing personal dynamics to interfere.

If you're struggling to find someone within your immediate network, consider joining a group or community focused on personal development or your specific goals. Online forums, social media groups, or local meetups can provide opportunities to connect with like-minded individuals who are also seeking accountability partners. These groups often have a shared sense of purpose, which can enhance the effectiveness of the partnership.

Accountability partnerships are not set in stone. It's perfectly okay to reassess and adjust the partnership if it's not working out as expected. Regularly check in with your partner about the effectiveness of your arrangement and be open to making changes if needed. If the partnership is no longer beneficial, it's better to address this openly and consider finding a new partner rather than continuing with an unproductive dynamic.

Choosing the right accountability partner can significantly impact your motivation and progress towards your goals. By finding someone who is reliable, honest, compatible, and supportive, you create a powerful ally in your journey. Establishing clear expectations, maintaining open communication, and being open to feedback are key components of a successful partnership. Remember, the goal of this relationship is to support and challenge each other towards continuous growth and achievement.

With the right accountability partner, you'll find yourself more motivated, focused, and equipped to overcome obstacles and reach your full potential.

3: Using Technology for Support

In our modern, digitally connected world, technology offers an array of tools that can significantly enhance your accountability and support system. By leveraging various apps and platforms, you can track your progress, share achievements, and receive virtual support, all of which contribute to maintaining motivation and achieving your goals.

Technology provides innovative solutions to the age-old challenge of staying accountable. Whether it's through goal-tracking apps, virtual support groups, or progress-sharing platforms, these tools can keep you connected and committed to your objectives. Let's explore how you can harness the power of technology to support your journey.

One of the primary benefits of using technology for support is the ability to track your goals and progress in real-time. Apps like Todoist, Trello, and Asana allow you to break down your goals into manageable tasks, set deadlines, and monitor your progress. These platforms offer visual tools, such as checklists and progress bars, which provide a clear overview of what you've accomplished and what remains to be done. By regularly updating your progress, you can maintain a sense of momentum and ensure that you're staying on track.

Another significant advantage of technology is the ability to share your progress and receive feedback. Social media platforms, such as Facebook, Instagram, and LinkedIn, allow you to connect with like-minded individuals and share your achievements. By posting updates about your goals and progress, you invite encouragement and constructive feedback from your network. This social reinforcement can boost your motivation and help you stay accountable to your commitments.

Virtual support groups and online communities are also invaluable resources for maintaining accountability. Platforms like Reddit, Discord, and specialized forums cater to various interests and goals, providing a space where you can connect with others who share your aspirations. These communities offer a supportive environment where you can share experiences, seek advice, and celebrate milestones. Engaging with a virtual support group can provide the encouragement and accountability you need to stay focused on your goals.

In addition to social platforms, there are numerous apps specifically designed to facilitate accountability and support. Apps like Habitica, Strides, and StickK use gamification to turn goal tracking into an engaging and motivating experience. Habitica, for example, transforms your tasks and goals into a role-playing game where you earn rewards for completing tasks and face consequences for falling short. Strides and StickK offer similar features, allowing you to set goals, track progress, and even wager money on your success to increase your commitment.

For those seeking more personalized support, coaching and mentoring platforms like Coach.me and BetterUp connect you with professional coaches who can provide guidance and accountability. These platforms offer one-on-one coaching sessions, goal-setting tools, and progress tracking features. By working with a coach, you receive tailored advice and support that can help you navigate challenges and stay motivated.

Video conferencing tools, such as Zoom, Skype, and Google Meet, also play a crucial role in maintaining accountability and support, especially in remote or hybrid work environments. These platforms enable you to have regular check-ins with your accountability partner, mentor, or support group, ensuring that you stay connected and engaged. Regular virtual meetings can help you stay focused on your goals and provide an opportunity to discuss progress, challenges, and strategies.

Another innovative way to leverage technology for support is through journaling and self-reflection apps. Apps like Day One, Journey, and Reflectly offer digital journaling tools that help you document your progress, reflect on your experiences, and track your growth. By regularly journaling about your goals and achievements, you gain insights into your progress and maintain a positive outlook. These apps often include features like prompts, mood tracking, and progress summaries, which can further enhance your self-awareness and motivation.

Furthermore, mindfulness and meditation apps like Headspace, Calm, and Insight Timer can support your mental well-being and resilience as you work towards your goals. These apps offer guided meditations, mindfulness exercises, and relaxation techniques that can help you manage stress, stay focused, and maintain a positive mindset. By incorporating mindfulness practices into your routine, you enhance your overall well-being and create a solid foundation for achieving your goals.

To maximize the benefits of technology, it's essential to choose the right tools that align with your preferences and goals. Consider the following tips when selecting and using technology for support:

1. Identify Your Needs: Determine what type of support you need—whether it's goal tracking, social reinforcement, professional coaching, or mental well-being. This will help you choose the most suitable apps and platforms.

2. Start Small: Begin with one or two tools and gradually incorporate more as needed. Starting small allows you to become familiar with the features and integrate them into your routine without feeling overwhelmed.

3. Stay Consistent: Regularly update your progress, engage with your support groups, and participate in coaching

sessions. Consistency is key to maintaining accountability and reaping the benefits of these tools.

4. Reflect and Adjust: Periodically review your progress and the effectiveness of the tools you're using. Adjust as necessary to ensure that they continue to meet your needs and support your goals.

Technology offers a wealth of resources to enhance your accountability and support system. By leveraging goal-tracking apps, social platforms, virtual support groups, coaching services, and mindfulness apps, you can stay connected, motivated, and committed to your goals. Embrace these digital tools as valuable allies on your journey towards personal and professional growth and watch as they help you achieve your aspirations with greater ease and confidence.

4: Setting Up Regular Check-Ins

Regular check-ins are essential for maintaining accountability and receiving ongoing support. This section discusses how to set up effective check-ins with your accountability partner or support network. We'll cover the frequency, structure, and content of these check-ins to ensure they are productive and motivating.

Maintaining regular check-ins is one of the most effective ways to stay on track with your goals. Whether you are working with an accountability partner, a mentor, or a support group, these check-ins provide a structured opportunity to reflect on your progress, address challenges, and stay motivated. Regular check-ins help to reinforce your commitment to your goals and ensure that you are consistently moving forward.

To set up regular check-ins, start by determining the frequency that works best for you and your accountability partner or support network. The frequency of check-ins can vary depending on the nature of your goals and the level of support you need. Some people find that weekly check-ins are ideal for maintaining momentum, while others may prefer bi-weekly or monthly check-ins. It's important to choose a frequency that allows you to stay engaged and receive the support you need without feeling overwhelmed.

Once you have established the frequency of your check-ins, it's important to create a structure that ensures these meetings are productive and focused. A well-structured check-in should include several key components:

Setting the Agenda

Start each check-in by setting an agenda. This can be a simple outline of the topics you want to discuss, such as your progress since the last check-in, any challenges you've encountered, and your goals for the upcoming period. Having a clear agenda helps to keep the check-in focused and ensures that you cover all important points.

Reviewing Progress

Begin the check-in by reviewing your progress since the last meeting. This is an opportunity to celebrate your successes and acknowledge the effort you've put in. Reflect on what has gone well and identify any factors that have contributed to your progress. Recognizing your achievements, no matter how small, can boost your motivation and reinforce your commitment to your goals.

Addressing Challenges

Next, discuss any challenges or obstacles you've faced since the last check-in. Be honest about the difficulties you've encountered and seek input from your accountability partner or support network on how to overcome these challenges. Brainstorming solutions together can provide new perspectives and strategies that you may not have considered on your own. Remember, the goal of these check-ins is to provide support and encouragement, so approach this discussion with a problem-solving mindset.

Setting New Goals

After addressing challenges, set new goals for the upcoming period. These goals should be specific, measurable, and achievable. Break down larger goals into smaller, manageable tasks that you can work on between check-ins. Setting clear, actionable goals gives you a sense of direction and purpose, helping you to stay focused and motivated.

Providing and Receiving Feedback

Constructive feedback is an important component of regular check-ins. Be open to receiving feedback from your accountability partner or support network and provide feedback in return. Feedback should be specific and focused on behaviours and actions rather than personal attributes. Use feedback as an opportunity to learn and grow, and to refine your approach to achieving your goals.

Celebrating Milestones

Take time to celebrate milestones and achievements during your check-ins. Acknowledging your progress and celebrating your successes, no matter how small, can boost your confidence and motivation. Celebrating milestones helps to reinforce positive behaviours and encourages you to continue working towards your goals.

Adjusting Goals and Strategies

As you review your progress and set new goals, be open to adjusting your goals and strategies as needed. Flexibility is key to maintaining momentum and staying motivated. If you find that certain goals are no longer relevant or achievable, don't be afraid to revise them. Adjusting your goals and strategies ensures that you remain focused on what is most important and allows you to respond to changing circumstances.

Maintaining Consistency

Consistency is crucial for maintaining the effectiveness of regular check-ins. Make a commitment to attend each check-in and encourage your accountability partner or support network to do the same. Consistency helps to build trust and accountability and ensures that you receive ongoing support and encouragement.

Building a Supportive Relationship

The relationship you build with your accountability partner or support network is foundational to the success of your check-ins. Foster a supportive and collaborative relationship based on mutual respect and trust. Be honest and transparent in your communication and approach each check-in with a positive and encouraging attitude. Building a strong, supportive relationship enhances the effectiveness of your check-ins and provides a sense of community and belonging.

Regular check-ins are a powerful tool for maintaining accountability and receiving ongoing support. By setting the agenda, reviewing progress, addressing challenges, setting new goals, providing and receiving feedback, celebrating milestones, adjusting goals and strategies, maintaining consistency, using technology to enhance check-ins, and building a supportive relationship, you can ensure that your check-ins are productive and motivating.

Regular check-ins also help to reinforce your commitment to your goals, provide valuable support and encouragement, and keep you on track to achieve your objectives.

5: Balancing Independence and Support

Balancing independence and support is essential for personal growth and success. While having a strong support system can provide invaluable guidance, encouragement, and accountability, maintaining a sense of independence ensures that you remain self-reliant and resilient. Finding the right balance between these two elements can empower you to achieve your goals while fostering personal development.

Support systems play a crucial role in our lives. They offer a safety net during challenging times, provide diverse perspectives, and help us stay motivated. Whether it's family, friends, mentors, or colleagues, having people who believe in you and your goals can significantly boost your confidence and drive. They can offer advice, share experiences, and provide constructive feedback that can help you navigate obstacles and stay on track.

However, while support is vital, it's equally important to cultivate independence. Independence fosters self-motivation, resilience, and a sense of ownership over your goals and achievements. When you rely too heavily on others, you might miss out on developing critical problem-solving skills and the confidence that comes from overcoming challenges on your own. Striking a balance between seeking support and maintaining independence is key to personal growth.

To achieve this balance, start by clearly defining your goals and responsibilities. Understand what you need to accomplish independently and where you can seek support. For instance, you might take full responsibility for researching and planning your project, while seeking feedback from a mentor to refine your ideas. This approach allows you to remain in control of your goals while leveraging the insights and experiences of others.

Developing self-awareness is also crucial. Regularly assess your progress and reflect on your strengths and areas for improvement. This self-awareness helps you understand when to seek support and when to rely on your abilities. It's essential to recognize your limitations without diminishing your capabilities. Embrace the idea that asking for help is not a sign of weakness but a strategic move to enhance your growth and success.

Effective communication is another key component of balancing independence and support. Clearly articulate your needs and expectations to your support network. Let them know how they can assist you without taking over your responsibilities. This clarity ensures that you receive the support you need while maintaining control over your goals. It's also important to express gratitude for the support you receive, reinforcing positive relationships and mutual respect.

Creating a structured plan can help you manage this balance effectively. Outline specific tasks that you will handle independently and identify areas where you will seek support. This plan provides a roadmap that keeps you accountable and focused. It also helps you allocate time and resources efficiently, ensuring that you remain productive and proactive.

Building resilience is another essential aspect of balancing independence and support. Resilience is the ability to bounce back from setbacks and challenges. By developing resilience, you enhance your capacity to handle difficulties independently while recognizing when to seek support. Practice resilience by setting realistic expectations, embracing failure as a learning opportunity, and staying adaptable in the face of change.

Remember that balancing independence and support is a dynamic process. As you progress towards your goals, your needs and circumstances may change. Regularly reassess your approach and make adjustments as necessary. Flexibility and adaptability are key to maintaining this balance over time.

One practical way to foster independence is by setting small, achievable goals. These goals provide opportunities to build confidence and competence incrementally. Each small success reinforces your ability to accomplish tasks independently, boosting your self-esteem and motivation. As you achieve these milestones, you'll find it easier to tackle larger challenges with a sense of assurance and determination.

Additionally, consider diversifying your support network. Different people can offer various perspectives, skills, and experiences. By engaging with a diverse group of supporters, you gain a broader range of insights and resources. This diversity can enrich your decision-making process and enhance your problem-solving abilities.

Balancing independence and support is essential for personal growth and success. While a strong support system provides invaluable guidance and encouragement, maintaining independence fosters self-motivation, resilience, and a sense of ownership over your goals. By clearly defining your responsibilities, developing self-awareness, communicating effectively, creating a structured plan, and building resilience, you can strike the right balance between these two elements. This balance empowers you to achieve your goals while fostering personal development, ultimately leading to a more fulfilling and successful life.

Chapter 8: Practicing Self-Compassion

"Now we'll focus on the importance of self-compassion and self-care. It will share techniques for managing stress, avoiding burnout, and being kind to yourself during difficult times.

Practicing self-compassion is essential for maintaining long-term motivation and confidence. Let's explore how you can integrate these practices into your life to support your ongoing well-being and success."

Synopsis

Now we'll focus on the essential practice of self-compassion. Being kind to yourself is crucial for maintaining motivation, building resilience, and fostering a positive self-image. This chapter will guide you through the importance of self-compassion and how to incorporate it into your daily life.

Understanding Self-Compassion

Self-compassion is about treating yourself with the same kindness and care you offer to others. We'll explore what self-compassion is and why it's essential for your well-being. This section will help you understand the difference between self-compassion and self-indulgence.

Identifying Self-Critical Thoughts

Many of us have an inner critic that can be harsh and judgmental. We'll discuss how to recognize self-critical thoughts and understand their impact on your self-esteem and motivation. This section will provide strategies to challenge and reframe these negative thoughts.

Developing a Self-Compassion Practice

Building a self-compassion practice involves intentional daily actions. We'll explore practical techniques such as mindfulness, self-compassion meditations, and journaling. This section will guide you in integrating these practices into your routine to foster a kinder relationship with yourself.

Healing Through Self-Compassion

Self-compassion can be a powerful tool for healing past wounds and traumas. We'll discuss how to use self-compassion to process difficult emotions and experiences. This section will provide insights on how to nurture yourself through challenging times.

Cultivating a Positive Self-Image

A positive self-image is built on self-compassion and self-acceptance. We'll explore how to shift your focus from self-criticism to self-appreciation. This section will offer exercises to help you recognize and celebrate your strengths and achievements.

Sustaining Self-Compassion Over Time

Maintaining self-compassion is a continuous journey. We'll discuss how to keep your self-compassion practice alive through ups and downs. This section will provide tips on staying committed to being kind to yourself, especially during challenging periods.

By practising self-compassion you'll have a deeper understanding of self-compassion and practical strategies to integrate it into your life. Remember, being kind to yourself is not a sign of weakness but a foundation for strength and resilience.

1: Understanding Self-Compassion

Understanding self-compassion is a transformative journey that leads to improved well-being and a healthier self-image. Self-compassion involves treating yourself with the same kindness, care, and understanding that you extend to others. It is a fundamental aspect of emotional health that enables you to navigate life's challenges with resilience and grace.

The concept of self-compassion can sometimes be misunderstood. Some might think it is synonymous with self-indulgence or making excuses for oneself. However, self-compassion is far from these misconceptions. It is not about letting yourself off the hook for mistakes or avoiding accountability. Instead, it is about recognizing that everyone makes mistakes and that imperfections are a part of the human experience.

Kristin Neff, a leading researcher on self-compassion, defines it through three main components: self-kindness, common humanity, and mindfulness. Self-kindness involves being gentle and understanding with yourself rather than harshly critical. Common humanity means recognizing that suffering and personal shortcomings are part of the shared human experience. Mindfulness entails being present with your feelings without over-identifying with them or suppressing them.

Self-compassion is essential for your well-being because it provides a foundation of emotional stability and resilience. When you are self-compassionate, you are more likely to bounce back from setbacks and failures. This is because you do not compound your suffering with self-criticism, but instead, you offer yourself comfort and support. This approach helps to reduce anxiety and depression, as you cultivate a more forgiving and understanding attitude toward yourself.

Be Gentle with Yourself

One of the key differences between self-compassion and self-indulgence is the intention behind your actions. Self-indulgence involves seeking short-term pleasure at the expense of long-term well-being. It might mean avoiding responsibilities or overindulging in unhealthy habits. On the other hand, self-compassion is about making choices that support your overall health and happiness, even if those choices involve some discomfort or effort in the short term.

To practice self-compassion, start by paying attention to your self-talk. Notice when you are being self-critical and intentionally replace those thoughts with kinder, more supportive ones. For example, if you catch yourself thinking, "I'm so stupid for making that mistake," try to reframe it to, "Everyone makes mistakes, and I can learn from this experience." This shift in perspective can significantly impact your emotional well-being.

Mindfulness plays a crucial role in self-compassion. It involves being aware of your thoughts and feelings without judgment. When you are mindful, you can acknowledge your suffering without being overwhelmed by it. This balanced approach allows you to respond to your struggles with compassion rather than avoidance or over-identification.

Another way to cultivate self-compassion is through self-care practices. Taking time to care for your physical, emotional, and mental health is an act of self-compassion.

This might include activities like regular exercise, healthy eating, sufficient sleep, and engaging in hobbies that bring you joy. It also means setting boundaries and saying no when necessary to protect your well-being.

Understanding the common humanity aspect of self-compassion can be incredibly freeing. Recognizing that everyone experiences difficulties and that you are not alone in your struggles can alleviate feelings of isolation and self-judgment. This understanding fosters a sense of connection with others, which is essential for emotional support and resilience.

It's okay to forgive yourself

Self-compassion also involves forgiveness. Holding onto past mistakes or perceived failures can lead to ongoing self-criticism and emotional pain. Forgiving yourself for these mistakes does not mean condoning them but rather accepting them as part of your growth and learning process. This forgiveness allows you to move forward without the burden of self-imposed guilt and shame.

Incorporating self-compassion into your daily life requires practice and commitment. It is not a one-time event but an ongoing process of nurturing a kind and supportive relationship with yourself. This might involve setting aside time each day for self-reflection, journaling about your experiences, or practicing guided self-compassion meditations.

Self-compassion is about treating yourself with kindness and understanding, recognizing that imperfections are part of the human experience, and responding to your struggles with mindfulness and care. It is a powerful tool for enhancing your emotional well-being, resilience, and overall quality of life. By practicing self-compassion, you can develop a healthier, more forgiving relationship with yourself, which is crucial for personal growth and happiness.

2: Identifying Self-Critical Thoughts

Many of us have an inner critic that can be harsh and judgmental. This inner critic often manifests as self-critical thoughts, which can significantly impact your self-esteem and motivation. Recognizing these thoughts is the first step towards addressing them and fostering a more compassionate and supportive inner dialogue.

Self-critical thoughts often stem from deeply ingrained beliefs about ourselves. These beliefs might have developed over time due to past experiences, societal pressures, or negative feedback from others. They can manifest in various forms, such as thoughts of not being good enough, fear of failure, or excessive self-doubt. These thoughts can be persistent and can influence how we perceive ourselves and our abilities.

To begin identifying self-critical thoughts, it's essential to develop self-awareness. Pay attention to your inner dialogue, especially in situations where you feel stressed, anxious, or discouraged. Notice the language you use when talking to yourself. Are your thoughts supportive and encouraging, or are they critical and demeaning? For example, after making a mistake, do you think, "I'm such an idiot," or do you say to yourself, "It's okay to make mistakes; I can learn from this"?

Journaling can be a powerful tool to help recognize self-critical thoughts. Set aside time each day to write down your thoughts and feelings. When you encounter a challenging situation, jot down your immediate reactions and the thoughts that arise. Over time, patterns may emerge, revealing recurring themes in your self-talk. This process helps you become more aware of how often and in what contexts self-critical thoughts appear.

Understanding the impact of self-critical thoughts is crucial. These thoughts can lead to a negative self-perception, lower self-esteem, and decreased motivation. When you constantly criticize yourself, it becomes challenging to believe in your abilities and take positive steps towards your goals. Self-critical thoughts can create a cycle of negativity, where you feel unworthy or incapable, leading to further self-doubt and inaction.

Challenge Thoughts That Don't Support The Best Version of Yourself

One effective strategy to challenge self-critical thoughts is to question their validity. Ask yourself whether these thoughts are based on facts or assumptions. For instance, if you think, "I'll never be successful," examine the evidence supporting this belief. Have you had successes in the past? Are there aspects of your life where you've achieved your goals? By challenging the accuracy of self-critical thoughts, you can begin to see them for what they are: unhelpful and often unfounded beliefs.

Reframing negative thoughts into more constructive ones is another powerful technique. Instead of thinking, "I'm terrible at this," try reframing it to, "I'm learning and improving each day." This shift in perspective can help you approach challenges with a growth mindset, viewing setbacks as opportunities for growth rather than as confirmations of inadequacy. Practice self-compassion by treating yourself with the same kindness and understanding you would offer a friend. When you make a mistake, remind yourself that everyone makes mistakes and that it's a natural part of the learning process.

Affirmations can also play a significant role in countering self-critical thoughts. Develop a list of positive affirmations that resonate with you and reflect your strengths and potential. Repeat these affirmations daily, especially during times of self-doubt. Affirmations such as "I am capable and resilient," "I trust myself to make the right decisions," or "I am worthy of success" can help shift your mindset towards a more positive and empowering direction.

Surrounding yourself with supportive and positive influences can further aid in challenging self-critical thoughts. Seek out friends, mentors, or support groups that encourage and uplift you. Their positive reinforcement can help counterbalance the negativity of your inner critic. Sharing your thoughts and experiences with others can also provide new perspectives and insights, helping you see yourself in a more positive light.

Identifying self-critical thoughts is a crucial step in fostering a healthier self-image and improving your motivation. By developing self-awareness, questioning the validity of these thoughts, reframing them, and practicing self-compassion, you can challenge the negative beliefs that hold you back.

Changing your inner dialogue takes time and effort, but with persistence and support, you can cultivate a more positive and empowering mindset. Embrace the journey of self-discovery and growth and be kind to yourself along the way.

3: Developing a Self-Compassion Practice

Developing a self-compassion practice is an essential step towards fostering a kinder and more supportive relationship with yourself. This practice involves intentional daily actions that nurture self-love and understanding, helping you to overcome self-doubt and build a resilient mindset. Let's explore some practical techniques such as mindfulness, self-compassion meditations, and journaling, and how to integrate these practices into your routine.

Self-compassion is about treating yourself with the same kindness and care that you would offer to a close friend. It involves recognizing your own suffering, understanding that everyone makes mistakes, and being gentle with yourself during difficult times. Research has shown that self-compassion can lead to greater emotional resilience, reduced anxiety, and overall well-being. By cultivating self-compassion, you can break free from the cycle of self-criticism and develop a more positive self-image.

Mindfulness and Self-Compassion

Mindfulness is the practice of being present and fully engaged with whatever you are doing in the moment. It involves paying attention to your thoughts, feelings, and sensations without judgment. Mindfulness can help you become more aware of your inner critic and create space to respond with compassion rather than harshness.

Start by setting aside a few minutes each day to practice mindfulness. Sit quietly, close your eyes, and focus on your breath. Notice any thoughts that arise and gently bring your attention back to your breath. As you practice, you will begin to notice patterns in your thinking and how often self-critical thoughts appear. Use this awareness to replace negative thoughts with compassionate ones. For example, if you catch yourself thinking, "I'm not good enough," gently reframe it to, "I'm doing my best, and that's enough."

Meditation is a powerful tool for developing self-compassion. There are specific meditations designed to cultivate feelings of kindness and compassion towards yourself. One such practice is the "Loving-Kindness Meditation."

To begin, find a quiet place where you won't be disturbed. Sit comfortably and close your eyes. Start by focusing on your breath, allowing your mind to settle. Then, recall phrases that evoke feelings of compassion, such as "May I be happy," "May I be healthy," "May I be safe," and "May I live with ease." Repeat these phrases silently, directing them towards yourself. Allow the feelings of kindness and compassion to grow with each repetition.

Regularly practicing loving-kindness meditation can help you develop a more compassionate inner dialogue and reduce self-criticism. It can also create a sense of connectedness with others, as you extend these wishes to friends, family, and even those with whom you have conflicts.

Journaling for Self-Compassion

Journaling is another effective way to cultivate self-compassion. Writing down your thoughts and feelings can help you process emotions and gain perspective. Use your journal to reflect on experiences, identify patterns of self-critical thinking, and practice self-compassionate responses.

Here are some journaling prompts to get you started:

Write about a recent situation where you were hard on yourself. How could you respond with more compassion next time?

List three things you appreciate about yourself. Reflect on how these qualities have positively impacted your life.

Describe a time when you showed compassion to someone else. How can you apply that same kindness to yourself?

Set aside a few minutes each day or week to write in your journal. This practice can help you develop a habit of self-reflection and self-kindness, reinforcing your commitment to self-compassion.

Integrating Self-Compassion into Your Routine

To make self-compassion a regular part of your life, find ways to integrate it into your daily routine. Here are some practical tips:

Morning Rituals: Start your day with a self-compassion practice, such as a short meditation or setting a compassionate intention for the day.

Mindful Breaks: Take mindful breaks throughout the day to check in with yourself. Use these moments to practice deep breathing or repeat a self-compassionate mantra.

Evening Reflection: End your day with a self-compassionate reflection. Write in your journal about your experiences, acknowledge your efforts, and remind yourself of your inherent worth.

By incorporating these practices into your routine, you can create a supportive environment that fosters self-compassion and helps you navigate life's challenges with greater resilience and kindness.

Developing a self-compassion practice is a journey that requires patience and consistency. Remember, it's not about achieving perfection but rather about making progress towards a more compassionate and loving relationship with yourself. Embrace this journey with an open heart and a willingness to grow, and you'll find that self-compassion becomes a natural and empowering part of your life.

4: Healing Through Self-Compassion

Healing is a deeply personal journey, and incorporating self-compassion into this process can be transformative. Self-compassion involves treating yourself with the same kindness, care, and understanding that you would offer a close friend. When dealing with past wounds and traumas, self-compassion becomes a crucial tool for navigating the healing process.

Self-compassion allows you to acknowledge your pain without judgment. It creates a safe space for you to process difficult emotions and experiences. By accepting your suffering and treating yourself with kindness, you can begin to heal and move forward. This approach contrasts sharply with the harsh self-criticism that often accompanies trauma, which can exacerbate feelings of shame and guilt.

A fundamental aspect of self-compassion is mindfulness. Mindfulness involves being present with your experiences without becoming overwhelmed by them. It means observing your thoughts and feelings without judgment. When applied to healing, mindfulness allows you to acknowledge your pain and trauma without being consumed by it. This awareness is the first step in creating a compassionate space for healing.

One practical way to cultivate mindfulness and self-compassion is through meditation. Self-compassion meditations often include guided practices that help you focus on treating yourself with kindness. These meditations can involve visualizing yourself offering comfort and support to a younger version of yourself or repeating affirmations that reinforce your worth and resilience. Regular practice can build a habit of self-compassion that extends beyond meditation and into your daily life.

Journaling is another powerful tool for self-compassion and healing. Writing about your experiences allows you to process and understand them better. It can also serve as a way to practice self-compassion by reflecting on your strengths and acknowledging your progress. Try dedicating a section of your journal to self-compassionate reflections. Write about moments when you showed yourself kindness or explore how you can bring more compassion into your life.

Your Unconscious Mind Believes Everything You Say

It's also important to recognize the impact of self-talk on your healing journey. Negative self-talk can hinder your progress by reinforcing feelings of inadequacy and self-blame. Transforming this inner dialogue requires conscious effort and practice. Start by identifying negative self-talk patterns and challenging them. Replace harsh criticisms with gentle, supportive affirmations. For instance, instead of thinking, "I should have done better," try saying, "I'm doing my best, and that's enough."

Connecting with others can also enhance your self-compassion practice. Sharing your experiences with trusted friends, family members, or support groups can provide comfort and validation. These connections remind you that you are not alone in your struggles and that others have faced similar challenges. This sense of shared humanity is a core component of self-compassion, as it reinforces the understanding that suffering is a universal experience.

Another key element of healing through self-compassion is forgiveness. Forgiving yourself for past mistakes and perceived failures is essential for moving forward. This doesn't mean excusing harmful behaviour but rather acknowledging that everyone makes mistakes and deserves compassion. Forgiveness allows you to release the burden of guilt and shame, opening the door to healing.

Engaging in activities that bring you joy, and relaxation is also crucial for self-compassionate healing. Whether it's spending time in nature, pursuing a hobby, or practicing creative expression, these activities can provide a much-needed respite from the intensity of the healing process.

They also reinforce the idea that you deserve care and kindness.

It's important to be patient with yourself as you navigate this journey. Healing is not a linear process, and there will be setbacks along the way. During these times, remind yourself that it's okay to feel vulnerable and that self-compassion is about being kind to yourself, especially when things are tough. Celebrate your progress, no matter how small, and acknowledge the courage it takes to face your pain and work towards healing.

Consider seeking professional support if needed. Therapists and counsellors trained in trauma and self-compassion can provide valuable guidance and support. They can help you develop personalized strategies for incorporating self-compassion into your healing journey and address any challenges you may encounter.

Self-compassion is a powerful tool for healing past wounds and traumas. By treating yourself with kindness and understanding, you create a nurturing environment for processing difficult emotions and experiences. Through mindfulness, meditation, journaling, positive self-talk, connection with others, forgiveness, and engaging in joyful activities, you can cultivate a self-compassionate practice that supports your healing journey. Remember to be patient and gentle with yourself, celebrating your progress and seeking support when needed.

5: Cultivating a Positive Self-Image

A positive self-image is rooted in self-compassion and self-acceptance, providing a foundation for personal growth and resilience. Shifting focus from self-criticism to self-appreciation involves deliberate, consistent effort and a change in mindset. Here, we explore various strategies to help you recognize and celebrate your strengths and achievements, fostering a healthier and more positive self-image.

Self-image is the perception you have of yourself, encompassing your beliefs about your appearance, abilities, and overall worth. It is shaped by experiences, interactions with others, and internal reflections. A positive self-image means viewing yourself with kindness and recognizing your inherent value, independent of external validation or accomplishments. This healthy perspective allows you to approach life with greater confidence and resilience, enhancing your ability to pursue goals and overcome challenges.

Self-compassion involves treating yourself with the same kindness and understanding you would offer a close friend. It means acknowledging your flaws and mistakes without harsh judgment. When you practice self-compassion, you create a nurturing environment that supports growth and learning. This compassionate approach counteracts the negative effects of self-criticism, which can erode self-esteem and hinder progress. By embracing self-compassion, you lay the groundwork for a more positive self-image.

Shifting Focus from Self-Criticism to Self-Appreciation

Self-criticism is a common barrier to a positive self-image. It involves focusing on perceived shortcomings and failures, often leading to feelings of inadequacy and self-doubt. To cultivate a positive self-image, it is essential to shift this focus towards self-appreciation. This shift involves recognizing and celebrating your strengths, achievements, and positive qualities. By consciously directing your attention to these aspects, you can reframe your self-perception and build a more balanced and affirming view of yourself.

Strategies for Cultivating a Positive Self-Image

1. Practicing Gratitude

Gratitude is a powerful tool for fostering a positive self-image. Regularly reflecting on what you are grateful for helps you appreciate the positive aspects of your life and yourself. Consider keeping a gratitude journal where you list things you appreciate about yourself each day. This practice reinforces positive self-perception and helps you focus on your strengths and accomplishments.

2. Positive Affirmations

Positive affirmations are statements that reinforce positive beliefs about yourself. They counteract negative self-talk and help reprogram your subconscious mind to adopt a more positive outlook. Create a list of affirmations that resonate with you, such as "I am capable," "I deserve success," or "I am worthy of love and respect." Repeat these affirmations daily, especially during moments of self-doubt.

3. Mindfulness and Self-Reflection

Mindfulness involves being present and aware of your thoughts and feelings without judgment. Practicing mindfulness can help you observe self-critical thoughts as they arise and consciously choose to redirect your focus to more positive and constructive thoughts. Incorporate mindfulness practices such as meditation, deep breathing, or mindful walking into your daily routine to enhance self-awareness and foster a positive self-image.

4. Celebrating Achievements

Acknowledge and celebrate your achievements, no matter how small they may seem. Recognizing your accomplishments reinforces a positive self-image and motivates you to continue striving towards your goals. Create a "success log" where you document your achievements, progress, and moments of pride. Review this log regularly to remind yourself of your capabilities and growth.

5. Seeking Positive Feedback

Constructive feedback from others can provide valuable insights into your strengths and areas for improvement. Seek feedback from trusted friends, mentors, or colleagues who can offer positive and balanced perspectives. Use this feedback to reinforce your self-appreciation and identify areas where you can continue to grow and develop.

Overcoming Barriers to a Positive Self-Image

Cultivating a positive self-image is an ongoing process that requires patience and persistence. Be aware of potential barriers, such as deeply ingrained negative beliefs, societal pressures, and comparison with others. Addressing these barriers involves challenging and reframing negative beliefs, setting healthy boundaries, and focusing on your unique journey and progress. Remember, building a positive self-image is not about perfection but about embracing your authentic self with kindness and appreciation.

To maintain a positive self-image, integrate self-appreciation into your daily life. Start each day with a positive affirmation, practice gratitude throughout the day, and reflect on your achievements in the evening. Surround yourself with supportive and uplifting influences, whether through relationships, books, or media. By consistently nurturing self-appreciation, you can build a resilient and positive self-image that supports your overall well-being and confidence.

Cultivating a positive self-image is a transformative journey that empowers you to embrace your true self with compassion and appreciation. By shifting your focus from self-criticism to self-appreciation, you can develop a healthier and more positive self-perception. Incorporate practices such as gratitude, positive affirmations, mindfulness, and celebrating achievements into your routine to reinforce a positive self-image. Remember, you are worthy of love, respect, and recognition, and by cultivating a positive self-image, you can unlock your full potential and thrive in all aspects of life.

6: Sustaining Self-Compassion Over Time

Sustaining self-compassion over time is a continuous and evolving journey that requires commitment, patience, and self-awareness. Maintaining a kind and nurturing relationship with yourself, especially during challenging times, is crucial for your overall well-being and resilience. In this section, we will explore various strategies to keep your self-compassion practice alive and thriving through life's ups and downs.

Self-compassion is the practice of treating yourself with the same kindness, care, and understanding that you would offer to a friend. It involves recognizing your own suffering, responding to it with warmth and support, and acknowledging that suffering is a shared human experience. This practice is not about self-indulgence or letting yourself off the hook for mistakes; rather, it's about fostering a healthy, nurturing relationship with yourself.

To sustain self-compassion over time, it's important to integrate it into your daily routine. Start by setting aside a few moments each day to check in with yourself. This can be as simple as taking a few deep breaths and asking yourself how you're feeling. Acknowledge your emotions without judgment and offer yourself kind words of support. This daily practice helps to build a habit of self-compassion that becomes second nature over time.

Another effective strategy is to practice mindfulness. Mindfulness involves being present in the moment and observing your thoughts and feelings without judgment. By cultivating mindfulness, you can become more aware of your inner critic and recognize when self-critical thoughts arise. When you notice these thoughts, gently redirect your focus to self-compassionate thoughts. For example, if you find yourself thinking, "I'm not good enough," replace it with, "I'm doing my best, and that's enough."

Journaling can also be a powerful tool for sustaining self-compassion. Take time each day to write about your experiences, emotions, and thoughts. Reflect on moments when you were kind to yourself and when you struggled with self-criticism. Writing about these experiences can help you gain insight into your patterns and identify areas where you can cultivate more self-compassion. Use your journal as a safe space to explore your feelings and practice self-kindness.

It's important to surround yourself with supportive influences that reinforce your self-compassion practice. Seek out relationships with people who uplift and encourage you. Share your journey with trusted friends, family members, or a therapist who can provide validation and support. Additionally, consume media that promotes self-compassion and positive self-esteem. Books, podcasts, and online communities focused on self-compassion can provide valuable insights and inspiration.

During challenging times, it's essential to be particularly vigilant about maintaining your self-compassion practice. When faced with difficulties, remind yourself that it's okay to struggle and that you deserve kindness and support. Create a self-care plan that includes activities that nourish your mind, body, and spirit. This might include taking breaks, engaging in physical activity, practicing relaxation techniques, or spending time in nature. Prioritize self-care and make it a non-negotiable part of your routine.

One powerful way to sustain self-compassion is through self-compassionate meditations. These guided practices can help you develop a deeper sense of kindness and understanding towards yourself. There are many resources available online, including guided meditations and mindfulness apps, that can support your practice. Regular meditation can help you build a strong foundation of self-compassion that you can draw upon during difficult times.

It's also helpful to remind yourself of the benefits of self-compassion. Research has shown that self-compassion is associated with numerous positive outcomes, including reduced anxiety and depression, greater emotional resilience, and improved overall well-being. By focusing on these benefits, you can stay motivated to continue your self-compassion practice, even when it's challenging.

Sustaining self-compassion is a lifelong journey. There will be times when you falter or find it difficult to be kind to yourself, and that's okay. The key is to approach these moments with the same compassion and understanding that you would offer to a friend. Acknowledge your struggles, forgive yourself, and recommit to your practice. Over time, you will develop a more compassionate and nurturing relationship with yourself that supports your well-being and resilience.

Maintaining self-compassion over time requires intentional effort and commitment. By integrating self-compassion into your daily routine, practicing mindfulness, journaling, surrounding yourself with supportive influences, prioritizing self-care, engaging in self-compassionate meditations, and reminding yourself of the benefits, you can cultivate a lasting and nurturing relationship with yourself. Remember that this journey is ongoing and that every step you take towards self-compassion is a step towards greater well-being and resilience.

Chapter 9: Measuring and Celebrating Progress

"Discovering the importance of tracking your progress and celebrating achievements is essential. This chapter will guide you through effective methods for measuring your success, reflecting on your growth, and adjusting your goals when necessary.

Celebrating your progress not only reinforces positive behaviour but also boosts your self-confidence. Let's explore how to make this a rewarding part of your journey together."

Synopsis

It's important to focus on measuring your progress and celebrating your achievements. Recognizing and honouring your progress is essential for maintaining motivation and building confidence. With empathy and understanding, I'll guide you through practical ways to track your accomplishments and celebrate your journey.

The Importance of Tracking Progress

Tracking your progress helps you stay motivated and focused. We'll explore why it's essential to measure your achievements and how it can boost your confidence. This section will provide insights into the benefits of regular progress reviews.

Setting Milestones and Benchmarks

Breaking down your goals into smaller milestones makes them more manageable and less overwhelming. We'll discuss how to set effective milestones and benchmarks that mark significant points in your journey. This section will help you create a clear roadmap to success.

Reflecting on Your Achievements

Reflection is a powerful tool for growth and motivation. We'll discuss the importance of regularly reflecting on your achievements and what you've learned. This section will offer techniques for meaningful reflection, such as writing prompts and guided questions.

Celebrating Small Wins

Celebrating small wins is crucial for maintaining motivation. We'll explore ways to celebrate your achievements, both big and small, and how to make these celebrations meaningful. This section will provide ideas for rewards and recognition that reinforce positive behaviour.

Adjusting Goals and Plans

As you progress, it's important to remain flexible and adjust your goals and plans as needed. We'll discuss how to evaluate your progress and make necessary adjustments to stay aligned with your long-term objectives. This section will help you stay adaptable and resilient.

By the end of Chapter 9, you'll have a solid understanding of how to measure and celebrate your progress effectively. Remember, every step forward is an accomplishment worth acknowledging. Let's work together to ensure that you recognize and honour your journey, staying motivated and confident as you move towards your goals.

1: The Importance of Tracking Progress

Tracking your progress is an essential aspect of maintaining motivation and achieving your goals. It provides a clear picture of where you stand, what you've accomplished, and what still needs to be done. By regularly monitoring your progress, you can stay focused, adjust your strategies as needed, and celebrate your achievements, all of which contribute to sustained motivation and confidence.

Tracking progress helps you understand the trajectory of your efforts. When you set goals, especially long-term ones, the journey can seem daunting. Breaking down these goals into smaller, manageable tasks and tracking your progress allows you to see incremental improvements. This visual representation of your journey can be incredibly motivating, as it shows that you are moving forward, even if the steps are small.

Moreover, tracking your progress helps you stay accountable. When you have a record of what you've done and what you still need to do, it's easier to hold yourself accountable. This accountability is a key factor in staying committed to your goals, as it prevents you from straying off course or procrastinating.

Boosting Confidence Through Progress Tracking

Seeing your progress can significantly boost your confidence. Each milestone you achieve, no matter how small, is a testament to your hard work and dedication. Celebrating these milestones reinforces the positive behaviour, encouraging you to continue pushing forward. This positive reinforcement is crucial for maintaining a high level of motivation.

Additionally, tracking progress helps you recognize patterns in your behaviour and productivity. By reviewing your progress, you can identify what strategies are working well and which ones need adjustment. This self-awareness allows you to make informed decisions about how to proceed, optimizing your efforts and increasing the likelihood of success.

Practical Tips for Effective Progress Tracking

To effectively track your progress, consider implementing the following strategies:

1. Set Clear Milestones: Break your goals down into smaller, achievable milestones. Each milestone should be specific, measurable, and time bound. This makes it easier to track and celebrate your progress.

2. Use a Tracking System: Utilize tools such as journals, apps, or spreadsheets to record your progress. Find a system that works best for you and is easy to update regularly.

3. Review Regularly: Schedule regular check-ins to review your progress. This could be weekly, bi-weekly, or monthly, depending on your goals. Regular reviews help you stay on track and make necessary adjustments.

4. Celebrate Achievements: Take time to celebrate your accomplishments, no matter how small. Acknowledge your hard work and reward yourself for reaching milestones. This could be as simple as treating yourself to something you enjoy or taking a moment to reflect on your success.

5. Adjust as Needed: Be flexible and open to adjusting your strategies if something isn't working. Tracking your progress provides valuable insights into what needs to be changed to stay on the path to success.

Overcoming Challenges in Progress Tracking

While tracking progress is beneficial, it can sometimes be challenging to maintain consistency. Life's demands and unforeseen obstacles can interfere with your tracking routine. To overcome these challenges, try the following approaches:

1. Simplify Your System: If tracking becomes overwhelming, simplify your system. Focus on key metrics

that are most relevant to your goals. Avoid overcomplicating the process with too many details.

2. Set Reminders: Use reminders to help you stay consistent with your tracking. Set alarms or calendar notifications to prompt you to update your progress regularly.

3. Find an Accountability Partner: Partner with someone who can help you stay accountable. Share your progress with them and encourage each other to stay on track.

4. Stay Positive: Keep a positive mindset, especially when progress is slow. Remember that any progress is still progress, and setbacks are a natural part of the journey.

Tracking your progress is a powerful tool for staying motivated, boosting confidence, and achieving your goals. By setting clear milestones, using an effective tracking system, and regularly reviewing your progress, you can maintain a clear sense of direction and purpose. Celebrating your achievements and being flexible with your strategies will help you stay committed and resilient, even in the face of challenges. Ultimately, tracking your progress not only keeps you focused on your goals but also reinforces the positive behaviours and efforts that lead to success.

2: Setting Milestones and Benchmarks

Setting milestones and benchmarks is a crucial strategy for achieving your goals, as it breaks down larger objectives into manageable steps, making them feel less overwhelming and more attainable. This approach provides a clear roadmap, guiding you through your journey and helping you track your progress effectively.

To begin with, it is essential to understand the difference between milestones and benchmarks. Milestones are significant points along your path to achieving a larger goal. They represent key achievements that indicate you are on the right track. For instance, if your goal is to write a book, milestones could include completing the outline, finishing the first draft, and submitting the manuscript for publication. Benchmarks, on the other hand, are smaller, measurable indicators of progress. They are the specific targets you set to monitor your advancement. Continuing with the book example, benchmarks could be writing a certain number of words per day or completing a chapter each week.

Define Your Goal

The first step in setting effective milestones and benchmarks is to clearly define your overarching goal. This goal should be specific, measurable, achievable, relevant, and time-bound (SMART). Once you have a well-defined goal, you can start breaking it down into smaller, more manageable parts. Think about the key stages or steps necessary to achieve your goal and use these as your milestones.

Next, establish benchmarks that will help you measure your progress towards each milestone. These benchmarks should be realistic and attainable within a short time frame. Setting too ambitious benchmarks can lead to frustration and demotivation if they are not met. Instead, aim for targets that challenge you but are still within reach. Regularly achieving these benchmarks provides a sense of accomplishment and keeps you motivated to continue.

A practical way to set milestones and benchmarks is to create a timeline or action plan. This visual representation of your journey can help you stay organized and focused. Divide your timeline into phases, with each phase culminating in a milestone. Within each phase, identify the specific benchmarks you need to hit to move forward. For example, if your goal is to launch a business, your timeline could include phases such as market research, product development, and marketing strategy. Benchmarks within these phases could be conducting customer surveys, finalizing the product design, and creating a social media campaign.

It is also important to remain flexible and adaptable. As you progress, you may encounter unforeseen challenges or opportunities that necessitate adjusting your milestones and benchmarks. Regularly review your progress and be willing to make changes to your plan as needed. This flexibility ensures that you stay on track and continue moving towards your goal, even if your initial plan requires modification.

Celebrating your achievements is another vital aspect of setting milestones and benchmarks. Each time you reach a milestone or meet a benchmark, take a moment to acknowledge your hard work and progress. This recognition reinforces positive behaviour and keeps you motivated. Celebrations do not have to be extravagant; they can be simple rewards such as taking a break, treating yourself to something special, or sharing your success with friends and family.

Setting milestones and benchmarks is an effective strategy for achieving your goals. It involves breaking down larger objectives into smaller, manageable steps, creating a clear roadmap, and regularly measuring your progress. By defining specific, achievable targets and celebrating your achievements, you can stay motivated and focused on your journey. Remember to remain flexible and adapt your plan as needed, ensuring continuous progress towards your ultimate goal.

3: *Reflecting on Your Achievements*

Reflecting on your achievements is an essential practice for personal growth and sustained motivation. When you take the time to acknowledge your progress, you not only celebrate your successes but also gain valuable insights into your journey. This reflective process can help you maintain a positive outlook, reinforce your commitment to your goals, and identify areas for improvement.

Reflection provides an opportunity to recognize the hard work and dedication that has led to your achievements. It allows you to appreciate the small victories that often go unnoticed in the hustle of daily life. By regularly reflecting on your accomplishments, you cultivate a sense of gratitude and pride in your efforts, which can boost your self-esteem and confidence. This positive reinforcement is crucial for maintaining motivation and staying focused on your goals.

One effective way to reflect on your achievements is through journaling. Keeping a journal dedicated to your progress can be a powerful tool for self-reflection. Set aside time each week to write about your accomplishments, no matter how small they may seem. Reflect on the challenges you faced and how you overcame them. Consider what strategies worked well and what you might do differently in the future. This practice not only helps you track your progress but also allows you to see patterns and trends in your behaviour and decision-making.

Ask Questions

Guided questions can also enhance your reflective practice. Ask yourself questions like, "What am I most proud of this week?" "What obstacles did I overcome?" "What did I learn from my experiences?" and "How can I apply these lessons moving forward?" These prompts can help you delve deeper into your reflections and uncover valuable insights. By exploring these questions, you gain a better understanding of your strengths and areas for growth, which can inform your future actions and decisions.

Another technique for meaningful reflection is to set aside time for regular check-ins with yourself. These check-ins can be daily, weekly, or monthly, depending on your preference. During these sessions, review your goals and assess your progress. Consider how far you've come and what steps you need to take next. This practice keeps you accountable and ensures that you stay aligned with your long-term objectives.

Reflecting on your achievements also involves celebrating your successes. Acknowledging your accomplishments, no matter how small, reinforces positive behaviour and motivates you to keep moving forward. Celebrate your wins in meaningful ways that resonate with you. This could be treating yourself to something special, sharing your success with a friend or mentor, or simply taking a moment to savor your achievement. Celebrations create positive associations with your efforts and encourage you to continue striving for your goals.

It's important to remember that reflection is not just about celebrating successes but also about learning from failures and setbacks. Reflecting on challenges and disappointments can provide valuable lessons that contribute to your growth. Instead of viewing failures as negative experiences, see them as opportunities for learning and improvement. Consider what went wrong, what you could have done differently, and how you can apply these insights to future endeavours. This mindset shift helps you build resilience and adaptability, essential qualities for long-term success.

Incorporating reflection into your routine requires consistency and intentionality. Make it a habit to set aside dedicated time for reflection, whether it's through journaling, guided questions, or regular check-ins. Treat this time as an essential part of your personal development journey. The more you practice reflection, the more natural it will become, and the greater the benefits you'll experience.

Reflecting on your achievements is a powerful practice for personal growth and motivation. It allows you to celebrate your successes, gain valuable insights, and learn from your experiences. By incorporating reflection into your routine, you reinforce positive behaviour, build resilience, and stay focused on your goals. Embrace this practice with an open mind and a willingness to learn, and you'll find that reflection can be a transformative tool on your journey to success.

4: Celebrating Small Wins

Celebrating small wins is a powerful and often overlooked strategy for maintaining motivation and fostering a positive mindset. These small victories are the stepping stones that lead to larger accomplishments, and recognizing them reinforces positive behaviour, keeps you engaged in your goals, and boosts your confidence. Celebrations don't have to be grand or extravagant; they just need to be meaningful and aligned with your personal values and interests.

First and foremost, it's essential to understand why celebrating small wins matters. Achieving big goals often requires a significant amount of time and effort, and without regular acknowledgment of progress, it's easy to become disheartened and lose motivation. Celebrating small wins creates a sense of immediate gratification, providing a mental and emotional boost that helps sustain your drive. Each small celebration acts as a positive reinforcement, making the journey towards your larger goals more enjoyable and manageable.

One way to celebrate small wins is through simple, everyday rewards. These can be as basic as taking a break to enjoy a cup of your favourite coffee, watching an episode of a TV show you love, or spending a few minutes in meditation or relaxation. The key is to choose rewards that feel like genuine treats to you and that you can look forward to. These small moments of joy and self-care can significantly enhance your overall sense of well-being and motivation.

Another effective way to celebrate is by sharing your achievements with others. Telling a friend, family member, or colleague about your progress can amplify the sense of accomplishment. Not only does it make the celebration more tangible, but it also allows you to receive positive feedback and encouragement from those who care about you. This social reinforcement can be incredibly motivating and can help you feel supported and appreciated in your efforts.

For more significant milestones, consider planning a special activity or event that you can look forward to. This could be a weekend getaway, a day trip to a favourite location, or a special meal at a restaurant you love. These bigger celebrations can serve as major motivational milestones that keep you focused and excited about the future. Knowing that there's a rewarding experience waiting for you can make the hard work feel more worthwhile.

Incorporating creative and personalized rewards can also make celebrations more meaningful. For example, if you enjoy reading, treating yourself to a new book can be a delightful way to celebrate a small win. If you're into fitness, buying new workout gear or booking a session with a personal trainer might be a rewarding acknowledgment of your progress. Tailoring rewards to your interests and passions ensures that each celebration feels special and relevant to you.

Journaling is another powerful tool for celebrating small wins. Keeping a journal of your achievements allows you to reflect on your progress and recognize your efforts. Writing down your successes, no matter how small, helps you internalize your accomplishments and provides a tangible record of your growth. On days when you're feeling discouraged, looking back at your journal can remind you of how far you've come and reignite your motivation.

In addition to individual celebrations, consider implementing a system of regular self-assessments and reflections. Setting aside time each week or month to review your progress and celebrate your wins can create a structured approach to recognizing your achievements. This practice not only keeps you aware of your growth but also helps you stay aligned with your goals and make necessary adjustments along the way.

It's important to note that celebrating small wins is not just about the external rewards but also about fostering a positive internal dialogue. Acknowledging your efforts and giving yourself credit for your hard work builds self-compassion and self-esteem. This positive self-talk reinforces your belief in your abilities and encourages a growth mindset, where you see challenges as opportunities for learning and improvement.

Celebrating small wins is a vital practice for sustaining motivation and fostering a positive mindset. By recognizing and rewarding your progress, you create a cycle of positive reinforcement that keeps you engaged and motivated. Whether through simple daily rewards, sharing achievements with others, planning special activities, or journaling, these celebrations make the journey towards your larger goals more enjoyable and fulfilling.

Every small step forward is a victory worth celebrating, and each celebration brings you one step closer to your ultimate success.

5: *Adjusting Goals and Plans*

Adjusting goals and plans is a critical component of long-term success. As we journey through life, our circumstances, priorities, and aspirations may change. Remaining flexible and adaptable ensures that we stay on course toward our overarching objectives, even as the path evolves. This ability to reassess and recalibrate our goals and plans not only keeps us aligned with our true desires but also fosters resilience and continuous growth.

The first step in adjusting your goals is to regularly evaluate your progress. Periodic reviews allow you to assess where you stand in relation to your initial objectives. Reflect on what you have achieved, the challenges you have faced, and the lessons you have learned. This self-assessment provides valuable insights into what is working well and what might need to be changed. It also helps you celebrate your progress, no matter how small, reinforcing your motivation and commitment.

When evaluating your goals, it's important to consider whether they still resonate with your current values and circumstances. Life is dynamic, and what seemed like a priority a few months ago might no longer hold the same significance. Ask yourself if your goals still align with your long-term vision and if they reflect your evolving passions and responsibilities. If you find that certain goals no longer serve you, it's okay to let them go or modify them to better suit your present situation.

Flexibility in goal setting involves being open to change and willing to adapt your plans as needed. This doesn't mean abandoning your goals at the first sign of difficulty but rather being pragmatic and realistic about what is achievable. For instance, if unforeseen obstacles arise, such as health issues or changes in your personal or professional life, you may need to adjust your timelines or break your goals into more manageable steps. This approach allows you to maintain momentum without feeling overwhelmed or discouraged.

Adapting your plans also means being receptive to new opportunities. Sometimes, life presents unexpected possibilities that can lead you toward even greater fulfilment and success. By staying open-minded and willing to explore new directions, you can take advantage of these opportunities and incorporate them into your revised goals.

This adaptability ensures that you remain proactive and forward-thinking, continuously evolving and growing.

One effective strategy for adjusting goals is to set flexible milestones. Instead of rigidly sticking to a predefined plan, create milestones that allow for adjustments based on your progress and circumstances. These milestones act as checkpoints where you can pause, reflect, and make any necessary changes. This iterative process keeps you engaged and responsive, ensuring that your goals remain relevant and attainable.

Another crucial aspect of adjusting goals and plans is to seek feedback and support. Share your goals and progress with trusted friends, mentors, or accountability partners who can provide valuable perspectives and encouragement. Their insights can help you identify blind spots, refine your strategies, and stay motivated. Additionally, having a support system fosters a sense of accountability, making it more likely that you will follow through with your plans.

Maintaining a growth mindset is essential when adjusting your goals. Embrace the idea that setbacks and challenges are opportunities for learning and growth. Rather than viewing adjustments as failures, see them as part of the natural process of achieving long-term success. This positive outlook will help you stay resilient and focused, even when faced with difficulties.

To stay adaptable, it's also helpful to develop a routine of regular reflection and planning. Set aside time each week or month to review your goals, assess your progress, and make any necessary adjustments. This practice not only keeps you aligned with your objectives but also reinforces the habit of continuous improvement. It ensures that you remain proactive and intentional in your pursuits, always ready to adapt and thrive.

Adjusting your goals and plans is a vital practice for sustained success and personal growth. By regularly evaluating your progress, remaining flexible, and seeking support, you can navigate the inevitable changes and challenges that arise. Embrace the process of adjustment as a natural and empowering aspect of your journey, allowing you to stay aligned with your true aspirations and continue moving forward with confidence and resilience.

Chapter 10: Sustaining Long-Term Success

"In the final chapter, we'll focus on sustaining the habits and strategies you've learned throughout the book. We'll share tips for continuous improvement, adapting to changes, and maintaining a growth mindset.

By sustaining these practices, you can ensure that your confidence and productivity gains are lasting. Let's work together to make these positive changes a permanent part of your life."

Synopsis

In this chapter, we'll focus on how to sustain the progress you've made and ensure long-term success. Maintaining your achievements and continuing to grow is a continuous journey. With empathy and understanding, we'll guide you through strategies to keep your momentum and stay committed to your goals.

Maintaining Healthy Habits

Healthy habits are the foundation of sustained success. We'll explore strategies for maintaining the positive habits you've developed and avoiding burnout. This section will cover topics such as self-care, work-life balance, and stress management.

Building Resilience

Resilience helps you bounce back from setbacks and stay focused on your goals. We'll discuss techniques for building and maintaining resilience, including mindfulness practices, positive self talk, and seeking support. This section will empower you to navigate challenges with confidence.

Continuing to Seek Support and Accountability

Ongoing support and accountability are crucial for long-term success. We'll talk about how to maintain and evolve your support network over time. This section will provide insights on staying connected with your accountability partners and mentors.

Celebrating Milestones and Successes

Celebrating your achievements keeps you motivated and reinforces positive behaviour. We'll explore ways to celebrate your milestones and successes in meaningful and fulfilling ways. This section will help you recognize your progress and stay inspired to achieve even more.

This will give you a comprehensive understanding of how to sustain your progress and continue growing. Remember, long-term success is a journey, not a destination. Which will ensure that you maintain your achievements and keep striving towards your goals with confidence and determination.

1: Maintaining Healthy Habits

Healthy habits are the cornerstone of sustained success. They provide the structure and stability needed to navigate life's challenges with resilience and grace. Maintaining these habits is crucial for achieving long-term goals without succumbing to burnout. This section will explore strategies for preserving the positive routines you've developed and ensuring they remain a consistent part of your life.

Self-care is not a luxury; it is a necessity. It's the foundation upon which all other habits are built. When you prioritize self-care, you replenish your energy and fortify your emotional resilience. This includes physical activities like regular exercise, a balanced diet, and adequate sleep. But self-care also encompasses mental and emotional practices such as mindfulness, relaxation techniques, and spending time with loved ones. By consistently integrating these practices into your routine, you ensure that you are always operating at your best.

Balancing Work and Life

Work-life balance is another critical aspect of maintaining healthy habits. In today's fast-paced world, it's easy to get caught up in work demands and neglect personal time. However, a balanced life is essential for long-term well-being. Establish clear boundaries between work and personal time. Make a conscious effort to disconnect from work during non-working hours and engage in activities that bring you joy and relaxation. This balance prevents burnout and keeps you motivated and productive over the long haul.

Stress is inevitable, but how you manage it can make all the difference. Developing effective stress management techniques is crucial for maintaining healthy habits. Practices such as deep breathing exercises, meditation, and yoga can help reduce stress levels. Additionally, engaging in hobbies, spending time in nature, and fostering social connections provide natural stress relief. By proactively managing stress, you prevent it from undermining your health and productivity.

Consistency is key when it comes to maintaining healthy habits. It's important to create a routine that is realistic and sustainable. Set specific, achievable goals and track your progress. Use tools like planners, habit trackers, or mobile apps to keep yourself accountable. Remember that it's normal to encounter setbacks. When you do, don't be too hard on yourself. Instead, acknowledge the setback, learn from it, and get back on track.

Adapting to Change

Life is unpredictable, and sometimes your routine will need to adapt. Flexibility is an important aspect of maintaining healthy habits. Be open to adjusting your routine as needed to accommodate new circumstances. This might mean finding alternative ways to exercise, adjusting your work schedule, or incorporating new stress management techniques. The key is to stay adaptable while keeping your core habits intact.

Recognizing and celebrating your progress is essential for maintaining motivation. Every small victory reinforces your commitment to your healthy habits. Take time to acknowledge your achievements, no matter how small. This could be as simple as rewarding yourself with a favourite treat, enjoying a relaxing activity, or sharing your success with a supportive friend. Celebrating small wins keeps you motivated and reminds you of the positive impact your habits have on your life.

Mindfulness and Reflection

Regular reflection helps you stay connected to your goals and assess your progress. Take time to reflect on your journey and the impact of your healthy habits. Mindfulness practices, such as journaling or meditation, can facilitate this reflection. By regularly checking in with yourself, you can identify areas for improvement and make necessary adjustments. This self-awareness ensures that your habits remain aligned with your overall well-being and goals.

Maintaining healthy habits is a continuous journey that requires commitment, flexibility, and self-compassion. By prioritizing self-care, balancing work and life, managing stress effectively, and staying consistent, you create a foundation for sustained success. Celebrate your progress, build a supportive network, and regularly reflect on your journey to ensure your habits remain a positive and integral part of your life. With these strategies, you can maintain the healthy habits that drive your success and well-being.

2: Building Resilience

Building resilience is a crucial skill that empowers you to navigate life's challenges with confidence and determination. Resilience helps you bounce back from setbacks and maintain focus on your goals, even when faced with obstacles. Developing resilience involves a combination of strategies that strengthen your mental and emotional fortitude, allowing you to persevere through difficult times.

One effective technique for building resilience is practicing mindfulness. Mindfulness involves staying present in the moment and observing your thoughts and feelings without judgment. By cultivating mindfulness, you can reduce stress, improve emotional regulation, and increase self-awareness. This practice helps you remain calm and cantered during challenging situations, making it easier to respond thoughtfully rather than react impulsively.

Turn the Negative into Positive

Positive self-talk is another powerful tool for enhancing resilience. The way you talk to yourself greatly influences your mindset and ability to cope with adversity. Replace negative, self-defeating thoughts with positive affirmations and constructive self-dialogue. For example, instead of thinking, "I can't do this," remind yourself, "I am capable and strong enough to handle this challenge." By consciously shifting your inner dialogue, you can boost your confidence and foster a resilient mindset.

Seeking support from others is also vital for building resilience. Surround yourself with a supportive network of friends, family, and mentors who can provide encouragement, guidance, and perspective. Sharing your struggles and successes with trusted individuals can help you feel less isolated and more understood. Additionally, seeking professional support from a therapist or counsellor can provide valuable tools and strategies for managing stress and building resilience.

Another key aspect of resilience is setting realistic and achievable goals. Break down your larger goals into smaller, manageable steps. This approach allows you to celebrate incremental progress and maintain motivation. Each small success reinforces your belief in your abilities and builds momentum towards achieving your larger objectives.

Practicing self-care is essential for maintaining resilience. Prioritize activities that nourish your physical, emotional, and mental well-being. This might include regular exercise, healthy eating, adequate sleep, and engaging in hobbies that bring you joy. Taking care of yourself ensures that you have the energy and resources needed to face challenges head-on.

Resilience also involves learning from setbacks and reframing them as opportunities for growth. Instead of viewing failures as reflections of your worth, see them as valuable lessons that contribute to your personal development. Ask yourself what you can learn from each experience and how you can apply these insights to future situations. This growth mindset fosters resilience by transforming obstacles into stepping stones for progress.

Maintaining a positive outlook is another important component of resilience. Focus on the aspects of your life that you can control and take proactive steps to improve your circumstances. Cultivate gratitude by regularly reflecting on the positive aspects of your life and expressing appreciation for them. A positive attitude can enhance your resilience by helping you stay hopeful and motivated, even during tough times.

It's also beneficial to develop problem-solving skills to enhance resilience. Approach challenges with a solution-oriented mindset, identifying potential actions and evaluating their outcomes. This proactive approach enables you to tackle problems effectively and reduces feelings of helplessness.

Building resilience is an ongoing process. Continuously evaluate and refine your strategies to ensure they remain effective. Stay committed to your resilience practices, even when life is going smoothly, so that you're prepared to handle future challenges with strength and confidence.

Resilience is a multifaceted skill that empowers you to overcome setbacks and stay focused on your goals. By practicing mindfulness, engaging in positive self-talk, seeking support, setting realistic goals, prioritizing self-care, learning from setbacks, maintaining a positive outlook, developing problem-solving skills, and committing to ongoing growth, you can build and sustain resilience over time. These strategies will help you navigate life's challenges with confidence, determination, and grace.

3: Continuing to Seek Support and Accountability

Maintaining ongoing support and accountability is vital for sustained success in achieving your goals and overcoming challenges. Whether you are just starting on your journey or are well on your way, having a reliable support network and accountability system can make a significant difference in your motivation, resilience, and overall progress.

Support and accountability are not static concepts; they evolve as you grow and your needs change. To ensure that you continue to benefit from these essential elements, it's important to be proactive in seeking out and nurturing your support network and accountability partnerships.

Support from friends, family, mentors, and peers can provide emotional encouragement, practical advice, and a sense of belonging. As you navigate the ups and downs of your journey, having people who believe in you and your potential can be incredibly reassuring. They can offer different perspectives, help you brainstorm solutions to problems, and celebrate your successes with you.

Continuing to seek support means regularly engaging with your support network. This could involve scheduling regular check-ins with mentors, joining new groups or communities related to your interests or goals, and being open to forming new connections that can provide fresh insights and encouragement.

Evolving Your Support Network

As you progress, your support needs may change. For instance, if you initially sought support for starting a new business, you might now need advice on scaling your operations. It's important to recognize when your current support network may need to be expanded or adjusted to meet your evolving goals.

Consider seeking out mentors or joining professional groups that align with your current stage of growth. Don't be afraid to reach out to new people who can offer specialized knowledge or experience that you currently lack. By continuously evolving your support network, you ensure that you have access to the resources and guidance necessary for your ongoing development.

Maintaining Accountability

Accountability keeps you focused and committed to your goals. When you know that someone else is tracking your progress and holding you to your commitments, you are more likely to stay on track and push through challenges. Accountability can come in many forms, from formal relationships with coaches or accountability partners to informal agreements with friends or colleagues.

To maintain accountability, establish clear, regular check-ins with your accountability partner. These check-ins should be structured and focused on discussing your progress, setbacks, and plans moving forward. Having a consistent schedule for these meetings can help keep you accountable and motivated.

Long-Term Benefits of Support and Accountability

The long term benefits of having a strong support network and accountability system are manifold. They include sustained motivation, increased resilience, and a greater likelihood of achieving your goals. Support and accountability help you stay focused, overcome obstacles, and maintain a positive mindset, even during challenging times.

Moreover, being part of a supportive community fosters a sense of belonging and mutual growth. As you benefit from the support and accountability of others, you also could give back and support others on their journeys. This reciprocal dynamic creates a thriving environment where everyone can grow and succeed together.

Continuing to seek support and accountability is essential for long-term success. By nurturing your support network, evolving it to meet your changing needs, and maintaining a robust accountability system, you can ensure that you stay motivated, focused, and resilient on your journey towards achieving your goals.

You don't have to go it alone—embrace the power of support and accountability to help you thrive.

4: Celebrating Milestones and Successes

Celebrating milestones and successes is a vital aspect of maintaining motivation and reinforcing positive behaviour. Recognizing your achievements helps you stay inspired and committed to your goals, providing a sense of accomplishment that propels you forward. This process not only validates your efforts but also creates a positive feedback loop that enhances your self-esteem and determination.

Celebrating milestones involves acknowledging both significant achievements and smaller, incremental progress. Often, we focus solely on the end goal, overlooking the numerous steps it takes to get there. Each small victory is a testament to your dedication and hard work, and celebrating these moments helps you appreciate the journey as much as the destination. By taking the time to recognize and honour your progress, you reinforce the behaviours and attitudes that contributed to your success.

One effective way to celebrate milestones is through personal rewards. These can range from simple pleasures, such as taking a relaxing bath or enjoying your favourite meal, to more substantial rewards like a weekend getaway or purchasing something you've been wanting. The key is to choose rewards that are meaningful to you and align with your values and interests. This personal connection to the reward enhances its impact and makes the celebration more fulfilling.

Sharing your achievements with others is another powerful way to celebrate. Whether it's with friends, family, or a supportive community, sharing your successes creates a sense of camaraderie and collective joy. It also provides an opportunity for others to acknowledge your efforts and offer their congratulations, which can further boost your morale and motivation. Additionally, celebrating with others can inspire them to pursue their own goals, creating a ripple effect of positivity and encouragement.

Creating a ritual or tradition around celebrating milestones can add an extra layer of significance to the process. For example, you might decide to write a letter to yourself every time you reach a significant milestone, reflecting on your journey and expressing gratitude for your progress. Alternatively, you could create a visual representation of your achievements, such as a scrapbook or a vision board, where you can document and revisit your successes. These rituals not only make the celebrations more memorable but also provide a tangible reminder of your growth and accomplishments.

While celebrating successes is important, it's equally crucial to maintain a balanced perspective. Success is not always linear, and setbacks are a natural part of any journey. When you encounter obstacles or face challenges, it's essential to practice self-compassion and resilience. Acknowledge the effort you've put in, even if the outcome wasn't as expected, and use these experiences as learning opportunities. By maintaining a positive and growth-oriented mindset, you can celebrate your perseverance and adaptability in the face of adversity.

Incorporating gratitude into your celebrations can further enhance their impact. Gratitude helps shift your focus from what you have yet to achieve to what you have already accomplished. Take time to reflect on the progress you've made, the support you've received, and the lessons you've learned along the way. Expressing gratitude, whether through journaling, meditation, or simply taking a moment to reflect, fosters a sense of contentment and appreciation that enriches your celebration.

Celebrating milestones and successes is a personal and individualized process. What matters most is that the celebration feels meaningful and authentic to you. There is no right or wrong way to celebrate; it's about finding what resonates with you and makes you feel valued and motivated. By honouring your achievements in a way that feels true to yourself, you reinforce your commitment to your goals and nurture a positive and empowering relationship with your progress.

By acknowledging your achievements, rewarding yourself meaningfully, sharing your successes with others, creating rituals, practicing self-compassion, incorporating gratitude, and personalizing your celebrations, you can enhance your sense of accomplishment and stay inspired to achieve even more.

Every step forward is worth celebrating, and each milestone is a testament to your dedication, resilience, and growth.

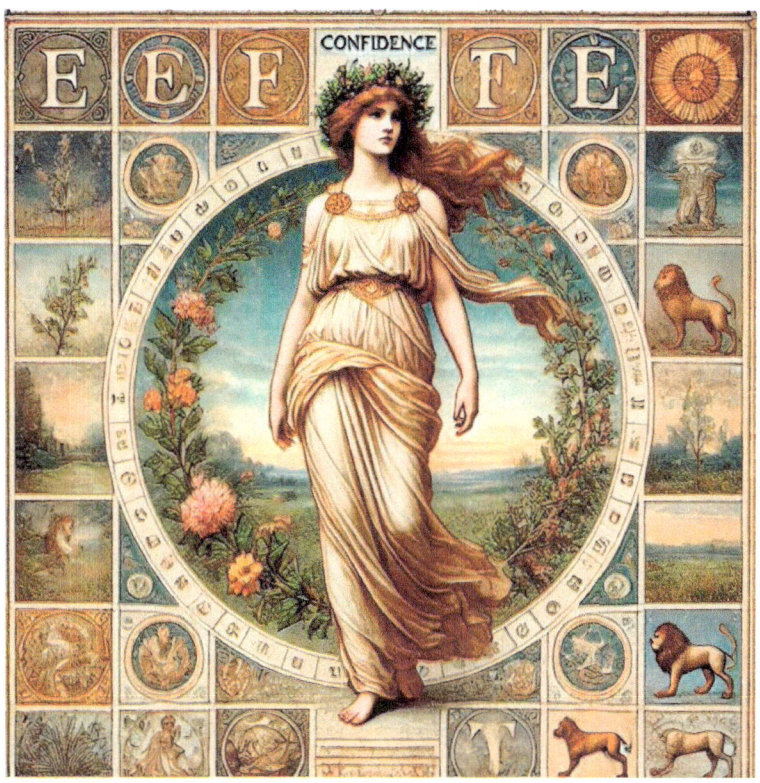

Conclusion: Embracing Your New Confidence

"Some final thoughts to remind you to embrace your newfound confidence and take on new challenges. Overcoming procrastination and self-doubt is a continuous journey, one that leads to a more fulfilling and productive life.

Celebrate the progress you've made and look forward to the opportunities ahead. This is just the beginning of your journey towards a more confident and empowered you"

As we reach the conclusion of our journey together, it's time to reflect on the transformative power of overcoming procrastination and self-doubt. Throughout this book, we have explored a variety of strategies and techniques designed to help you break free from the barriers that have held you back. Now, it's time to embrace your newfound confidence and take on the world with renewed vigour and determination.

Reflecting on the Journey

Let's take a moment to revisit the key concepts we've covered:

In Chapter 1, we discover that recognizing procrastination and self-doubt as silent saboteurs is the first step toward overcoming them. By understanding how these forces work together to hold us back, we can begin to dismantle the barriers they create. Embrace this insight as a powerful tool to unlock your full potential and move forward with renewed confidence and purpose.

Embracing Your New Confidence

With these insights and tools at your disposal, you are now equipped to face challenges head-on with a newfound confidence. Embracing this confidence is about more than just feeling good about yourself; it's about recognizing your worth, trusting in your abilities, and knowing that you have the power to achieve your goals.

The Continuous Journey

It's important to understand that overcoming procrastination and self-doubt is not a one-time achievement but a continuous journey. There will be times when old habits try to resurface, and moments when self-doubt creeps back in. However, armed with the knowledge and strategies from this book, you are prepared to address these challenges and continue moving forward.

Taking on New Challenges

As you move forward, don't be afraid to take on new challenges. Each challenge is an opportunity to apply what you've learned, to grow, and to build even more confidence. Remember, every small step you take is progress, and every success, no matter how small, is a victory worth celebrating.

Setting and Achieving Goals

One of the most powerful tools you now possess is the ability to set clear, achievable goals. Use this skill to your advantage. Whether your goals are personal, professional, or a mix of both, clearly defining what you want to achieve and creating a step-by-step plan will help you stay focused and motivated.

Developing Resilience

Building resilience is key to maintaining your progress. Life is unpredictable, and setbacks are inevitable. However, resilience allows you to bounce back from these setbacks and keep pushing forward.

Use the self-awareness techniques we discussed to stay in tune with your thoughts and emotions, and don't hesitate to adjust your plans as needed.

Building a Support System

Surround yourself with supportive people who encourage and believe in you. Whether it's friends, family, mentors, or support groups, having a network of positive influences can make a significant difference. They can provide encouragement during tough times, celebrate your successes, and help keep you accountable.

Celebrating Your Successes

Take the time to celebrate your successes, both big and small. Recognizing your achievements reinforces positive behaviour and boosts your self-confidence. It's easy to get caught up in the pursuit of the next goal, but don't forget to acknowledge how far you've come and the progress you've made.

Staying Motivated

Staying motivated is crucial for continued success. Remember to revisit your "why" – the reasons behind your goals and the vision you have for your life. Setting up a reward system and maintaining a positive attitude can help keep your motivation strong, even during challenging times.

Maintaining a Positive Mindset

Developing and maintaining a positive mindset is essential for overcoming self-doubt and staying on track. Practice gratitude, focus on your strengths, and use positive affirmations to reinforce your self-belief. A positive mindset not only boosts your confidence but also enhances your overall well-being.

Practicing Self-Compassion

Be kind to yourself throughout this journey. Practicing self-compassion means acknowledging that it's okay to make mistakes and understanding that setbacks are a natural part of the process. Treat yourself with the same kindness and understanding that you would offer a friend.

Continuing to Learn and Grow

Personal growth is a lifelong journey. Continue to seek out new knowledge, skills, and experiences that challenge you and contribute to your development. Stay curious and open-minded and embrace opportunities for learning and growth.

Final Thoughts

As we conclude this book, I want to leave you with a powerful message: You are capable, you are worthy, and you have the power to achieve your dreams. Overcoming procrastination and self-doubt is a journey that leads to a more fulfilling and productive life. Embrace your newfound confidence, take on new challenges, and continue to strive for the best version of yourself.

Remember, every step you take is progress. Celebrate your journey, stay motivated, and keep pushing forward. Your potential is limitless, and your future is bright. Embrace your new confidence, and let it guide you towards a life of success, happiness, and fulfilment.

Thank you for allowing 'overcoming self-doubt, empowering self-esteem' to be a part of your journey.

Here's to your continued growth and success.

Printed in Great Britain
by Amazon